The
Neanderthal
Legacy

The
Neanderthal
Legacy

Reawakening Our Genetic and Cultural Origins

Stan Gooch

Inner Traditions
Rochester, Vermont

Inner Traditions
One Park Street
Rochester, Vermont 05767
www.InnerTraditions.com

Library of Congress Cataloging-in-Publication Data
Gooch, Stan.
  The Neanderthal legacy : reawakening our genetic and cultural origins / Stan Gooch.
    p. cm.
  Summary: "A direct appeal for a revolution in our educational system to restore the connection with our Neanderthal heritage"—Provided by publisher.
  Includes bibliographical references and index.
  ISBN 978-1-59477-185-9 (pbk.)
  1. Neanderthals. 2. Cro-Magnons. 3. Human evolution. 4. Genetic psychology. 5. Brain—Evolution. I. Title.
  GN285.G65 2008
  569.9'86—dc22

14.95   2008003255

Printed and bound in the United States by Lake Book Manufacturing

10 9 8 7 6 5 4 3 2 1

Text design and layout by Jon Desautels
This book was typeset in Garamond, with Avant Garde Gothic as a display typeface.

To send correspondence to the author of this book, mail a first-class letter to the author c/o Inner Traditions • Bear & Company, One Park Street, Rochester, VT 05767, and we will forward the communication.

Contents

Publisher's Preface

STAN GOOCH, ONE OF the top experts in the world on the nature and mythology of the Neanderthals, was born in 1932 in London's docklands. His father was a private in the British army until he was discharged from active duty due to war wounds. His brother and sister were both physically handicapped from a rare genetic condition. He won a scholarship to Colfe's Grammar School and from there went on to get a degree in modern languages at King's College, London. He taught in a London grammar school for several years, during which time he also received a degree in psychology at Birkbeck College, London, and was appointed senior research psychologist at the National Children's Bureau. After coauthoring two textbooks on child development, Mr. Gooch decided to write full-time, despite being offered the directorship of the National Children's Bureau and the chair of psychology at Brunel University. He is the author of *Total Man, Personality and Evolution, The Neanderthal Question, The Paranormal, The Dream Culture of the Neanderthals, The Double Helix of the Mind, The Secret Life of Humans, The Origins of Psychic Phenomena,* and *Cities of Dreams.*

Mr. Gooch's working title for this book was *Mayday Mayday Fifty Percent of Our History Is Missing or Should That Be Fifty Percent of Our*

Psychology Is Missing—No, It's Both. This gives you a sense of the scope of this book, his latest work. It is a mass of information concerning our historical past and our current psychology that has been ignored by our academic and scientific establishments. Mr. Gooch has gathered the information over many decades of research from a variety of reliable sources. Some of the information has appeared in his earlier works.

A selected bibliography has been included along with citations for a few specific pieces of information. Unfortunately, at the time of publication, Mr. Gooch was not well enough to compile all the sources he used for the writing of this manuscript. On behalf of Mr. Gooch, we encourage you to read his earlier works, which include more complete source information.

PART ONE

Our Missing History

Chapter 1
Our Denial of Thirteen

MY NINE EARLIER BOOKS give many thousands of academic and scientific references to the material of this present book.

But in this present book I am making instead a simple and direct approach in particular to students—but equally to other intelligent individuals—asking them to go to their teachers, lecturers, and professors to ask them for their views and explanations of the mass of material involved.

But I have to say in advance, there will not *be* any explanations.

So to begin, students, your first question is: sir/madam, why is it that all leading and founding groups and structures in every civilization *worldwide,* both *past* and *present,* number thirteen?

So we have Christ and the twelve disciples; Odysseus and his twelve companions; Jacob and his twelve sons; Roland and the twelve peers of France; Hrolf and the twelve Berserks; Romulus and the twelve shepherds; the coven thirteen of the Druids; the king and the twelve knights of the Order of the Garter (may I just mention that the robes of the knights and the king were embroidered with 168 garters, which, plus the garter worn on the leg, gives 169—that is, 13 × 13?); King Arthur and his twelve knights of the Round Table (which turns out to be a zodiac with thirteen signs, by the way); Robin Hood and his twelve merry men (should I mention that Robin is the commonest name for a witch's familiar throughout Britain and is slang for penis?—sorry, I'm getting sidetracked into later matters); the judge and twelve jurors; Baiani and his twelve followers (they were the founders of the Australian Aborigine nation, of course—oh, you didn't know that); and so forth— and then we also have the thirteen Valkyries; Asgard, the seat of the Teutonic gods, divided into thirteen spheres; the gods of Valhalla, which originally numbered thirteen; the original thirteen tribes of Israel; the thirteen attributes that Orthodox Judaism even today accords to God; the thirteen Buddhas of the Indian pantheon; the thirteen mystical disks that surmount both Indian and Chinese pagodas; the thirteen sacred items found in many Chinese and Japanese temples; and that the most sacred number in Mexico is the number thirteen, that thirteen was also centrally revered among Incas, Aztecs, and Toltecs—and, in fact, by every tribe and people throughout Central, South, and North America—that's every tribe. (Gosh.)

I'll stop there for the moment. But what's clear from these items, sir/madam, is that the number thirteen is central to every culture and civilization throughout the whole world and the whole of human history. I'm wondering how and why that is the case. *Especially* in view of the fact that today, publicly, thirteen is the most hated, feared, and despised number that we have! Can you please explain this situation to me?

What—you didn't really *know* most of this material? And so you don't *have* any explanation?

(I'm not very encouraged by that, sir/madam.)

So what can we say about this?

Let's ask, for starters, does the number thirteen occur anywhere in nature? Yes, it does. But only in one context.

There are thirteen new moons/thirteen full moons in each alternate year.

Oh, did I say that was the only thirteen? Sorry, I should have pointed out that women menstruate/ovulate thirteen times in each alternate year.

Ah—but these "two different" items are in fact *one and the same item!*

First, even under modern living conditions, a majority of women menstruate around the new moon and ovulate around the full moon. The length of a lunar cycle is 29.53 days. The average human female cycle is 28 to 30 days. And so is the menstrual cycle of gibbons and orangutans. But *not* that of monkeys, which can be 10 days, 18 days, 23 days, whatever.

Further, as actual experiments have shown, a woman suffering from irregular periods can have them regularized by having a light on in a closet in the bedroom during certain nights of the month (that's the moon, of course). The woman's menstrual cycle regularizes at—guess what—29 days.

But there is a more crucial item still.

The length of a normal human pregnancy is 9×29.53 days—almost to the minute. Can I repeat that, sir/madam? *Almost to the minute.*

This last item (but, of course, along with the other evidence) is crucial *proof* that the human menstrual and pregnancy cycles are governed by the moon.

Two questions, sir/madam.

1. How and why did the menstrual cycle of humans (and some apes) become linked to the cycles of the moon—at this very, very late stage of evolution? Remember that monkeys, the apes' closest relatives, show no sign of such linkage. *How? Why?*
2. Why again are these amazing facts never debated or discussed in our schools, colleges, universities—or anywhere in the media? Why are they never mentioned?

Let's begin to pick up on a bit of detail in regard to the institutionalized thirteen in our various human cultures. We'll focus here specifically for the moment on the story of Christ and the twelve disciples, and the origins of Christianity.

Christ dies (at dusk) on Friday. Friday is Freija's day. And she is the Moon Goddess. He is resurrected three days later (and just in passing here, three is another important moon number—for instance, because the moon is absent from the sky for three nights of each cycle) (so is that why it takes Christ three days to re-arise?). He is resurrected on Monday. And Monday is, of course, Moon Day.

But more crucially still, Christ dies on the cross. *And the cross is the symbol for the moon in all pre-Christian cultures worldwide.* Shall I repeat that? In all pre-Christian cultures worldwide.

Christ dies at dusk on Friday; nightfall on Friday is the beginning of the Jewish Sabbath (which ends at dusk next day). (A little strange that the Jewish holy day *begins* at dusk?)

Now, guess what—and the following is absolutely crucial (although so is the cross and so on)—"Sabbath" (Hebrew *shabbat*) was originally the name of the monthly festival of the menstruation of the Moon Goddess.

Shall I say *that* once again, sir/madam?

The name of both the Christian and Jewish holy days, the Sabbath, is the name of the monthly festival of the menstruation of the Moon Goddess.

One more crucial *fact*. (Sorry I keep emphasizing the word *fact*.) The date of Easter, the festival of the death and resurrection of Christ, is to this day determined by the phases of the moon. That is why Easter is a moveable feast and changes its date from year to year. I'm going to say it once again. The date of the central Christian festival, Easter, is determined by the moon.

But when did you ever hear this astonishing fact discussed or debated, or explained? Never.

Anyway, we have already shown beyond any argument that central and crucial features of Christianity are derived from the ancient moon religion. And there'll be much more to say on that later in the book.

May we say here a bit more about the number thirteen? Yes, certainly.

We know, for example, that the astrological zodiac originally consisted of thirteen divisions and not twelve. This is again a fact because all the oldest stone zodiacs found (in Australia, North America, Israel, and so on) have thirteen divisions. (Incidentally, the Israeli example is on the floor of a synagogue, the Jewish equivalent of a church.) So there were thirteen months in the lunar year (as also confirmed, for example, in *The Ballad of the Curtal Friar:* "There be thirteen monthes in the year I say").

(With what justification are we saying the thirteen-sign zodiac is lunar—though how could it not be? Well, the spider will help confirm that for us later in the book!)

The ancient moon-worshippers—whom, again, we'll be saying much, much more about—had, in fact, hit on a brilliant idea. They were faced with the problem of equating the lunar year with the solar year, because the two do not agree (and that's why the moon date of Easter moves around in the solar year), of somehow fitting the two together.

What is known as the "stellar lunar" cycle is as follows: Every 28 days, the moon returns to the same point in the sky where it was last observed—that is, reaches the same point against the background of stars.

Now, 28×13 (hooray—we *can* still use our central moon number, chortled the moon worshippers) gives us 364 days. That 364 *plus 1,* of course, is, in fact, the "year and a day" so often mentioned in ancient legends and fairy stories—and gives us the 365 days of the solar year. That "and a day" is actually, once again, an extremely important item. As the shortest day of the year it is the day on which the sun dies—or, as I suggest, is sacrificed by the moon before she graciously resurrects him the next day.

Any more cultural thirteens?

The importance and significance of the pyramids of Egypt, Central America, and elsewhere cannot be disputed—and no one would do so.

But the point to make here is that the pyramid is the only structure (or shape found, anywhere among crystals) that has a total of—guess what—thirteen sides and edges (including base). Well, well.

And the Aztec Great Pyramid of the *Sun* (my italics) has 4 flights of 91 steps, giving us 4 × 91 = 364, the number of days in the lunar year. And 91 is, in any case, 7 × 13.

Both 4 and 7, incidentally, are also important moon numbers, and not just because 4 × 7 = 28. Four is derived from the four quarters of the moon—and as we shall see, the cross is, in fact, a stylized representation of the four quarters of the moon, which is why cross equals moon. As to seven, again, as we shall see, this is derived *not* principally from the seven stars of Ursa Major, the Great Bear (or Big Dipper), which indicates the still center of the heavens—but from the seven of the obscure little group of faint stars known as the Pleiades. And seven just turns out to be a central number of *all* religions *worldwide* (again the use of the words *all* and *worldwide*)—thus the Sabbath, Sunday, is the seventh day of the week. (Worth mentioning also that seven is the central/middle number between one and thirteen: 1, 2, 5, 4, 5, 6, 7, 8, 9, 10, 11, 12, 13; and that we have seven units of time: second/minute/hour/day/week/month/year.)

Oh, and I should have said earlier that Jewish boys reach manhood at the age of thirteen, when a special ceremony is held (the bar mitzvah). They are, of course, at that point 13 × 13 lunar months old. We already saw the combination of 13 × 13 in regard to the Order of the Garter.

And one more "little" item here. The Drachenloch altar in Switzerland, built by Neanderthals 75,000 years ago, contains—yes—thirteen bear skulls. Drachenloch means "lair of the dragon." And just to show we're not sidetracking, the Chinese call the movement of the moon as it snakes back and forth across the equator "the path of the dragon." Well, well.

Lots more to come about dragons later.

Chapter 2

Left: Left Out

WE HAVE ALREADY BEGUN to list the mass, the almost endless list, of *worldwide* items for which orthodoxy (a) has no explanation whatsoever; and, which it (b) either deliberately, or out of pure stupidity, chooses completely to ignore.

But at this point, perhaps I should begin to set out my own proposed scenario of explanation. This scenario deals, on one hand, with the mass of *cultural* mysteries—but on the other, also with the equal mass of *psychological* and *behavioral* enigmas for which, once again, orthodoxy has no explanation whatsoever (see part 2).

As we proceed, incidentally, I shall cite many recent discoveries and surveys that support, and often dramatically support, my views—and not one of which in any way contradicts them.

My scenario of our history and psychology, then, is that both culturally and genetically, we are a hybrid cross between the Neanderthal and Cro-Magnon varieties of early human.

Turning to specifics, my claim is that Neanderthal society was ruled and led by women and driven by sex—by which I mean totally promiscuous sex, also involving lesbianism and homosexuality. There was, in particular, no hint of pair-bonding whatsoever.

So, clearly, a totally wild and unfounded claim? Well, guess what?

The recently discovered bonobo chimpanzees of Africa are—yes—led by the females and practice totally promiscuous sex, including lesbianism and homosexuality. How lucky can I get! Much more lucky, as we shall see. (Incidentally, the bonobo chimps also practice pedophilia—there'll be more to say on pedophilia later.)

Further of my claims are that Neanderthals worshipped the moon and were at least seminocturnal. Also that Neanderthals were red-haired. And finally, that Neanderthals were left-handed.

Now, guess what? A Neanderthal carving of the Moon Goddess has been found in South Africa; it is 250,000 years old. (Yes—250,000.) Well, lucky me.

I was the only person in the world to claim that Neanderthals had red hair—that was back in 1989, in my book *Cities of Dreams*. In 2001, the Oxford Institute of Molecular Biology announced—Neanderthals had red hair. Lucky, lucky me again. (The U.K. *Times* newspaper did have the decency to write an article pointing out that I had got there first.)

Just one more point on this subject. Recent studies have now shown that redheads are the most sexually active of all human groups! That finding, of course, does no harm whatsoever to my claims about the Neanderthals' sexuality—quite the reverse, obviously.

But my "luck" goes on and on. Another recent study has shown that left-handedness is much more common among lesbians and homosexuals than in the general population! And yet another survey, that left-handed adults are, on average, shorter than right-handed adults. Neanderthals were, of course, much shorter than Cro-Magnons, as is well known—details on that later.

Of course, neither of these last two statements (or earlier statements) actually *proves* my claims in regard to Neanderthals. But they do them no harm whatsoever—quite the reverse.

Lastly, a tribe has been discovered in Siberia 66 percent of whom are left-handed! Scientists suggest that this dramatic level of left-handedness is an adaptation to extreme cold. Neanderthal, of course, lived through more than one ice age . . .

Now, as to the Cro-Magnons, I propose that their society was ruled and led by the males, and that one male bonded with one female for life (as is, of course, the case with Asian gibbons). Also that Cro-Magnons were creatures of daylight and the open plains, and that they worshipped the sun and were right-handed.

The above are, for the moment, some of my own specific claims concerning the two varieties of early humans.

But we already also *know* the following. These are agreed *facts*.

The classic Neanderthal was short in height, males an average five feet, four inches tall. The male was barrel-bodied, the so-called pyknic body type, and had a big toe shorter than the second toe. The back of the Neanderthal's head, the occiput, was extended (housing a much larger cerebellum than that possessed by Cro-Magnons), giving the so-called long head. The Neanderthal also had a backward-sloping forehead and very heavily armored jutting brow ridges. The chin was recessive, but the mouth large and protruding (prognathous). The Neanderthal's eye sockets were large (see figure 2.1). (This particular feature is, of course, regularly found in nocturnal creatures—but as far as I'm aware, nobody apart from myself has suggested that Neanderthals were nocturnal.)

Cro-Magnons were tall. Initial figures proposed that males were an average of six feet in height, but this figure was subsequently modified—to five feet, ten inches. The male's build was athletic—broad shoulders with narrow hips. The back of the head was flat or slightly rounded, the forehead high and straight. The brow-ridges were flat, as was the mouth. The chin, however, was strong and often projecting (see figure 2.2).

The Cro-Magnon male's height and athletic build very much suggest that he was a creature of the open plains and a hunter. The Neanderthal's short and barrel-bodied build is much more suited to life in the jungle or forests. Neanderthals therefore were more likely "gatherers" (and I will suggest later that they were, initially, at least, largely if not completely vegetarian).

Figure 2.1. Skull of a Neanderthal from Rhodesia (40,000 years BP [before the present]). Note the very heavily armored brow ridges and the very large eye sockets, typical of nocturnal creatures. These are the people who excavated the red ochre mines of southern Africa, no doubt by moonlight.

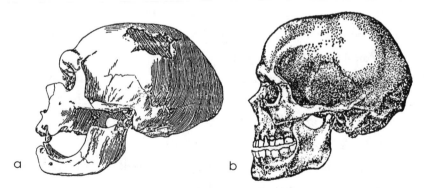

a   b

Figure 2.2. Skulls of (a) a Neanderthal man and (b) a Cro-Magnon man. Note the backward-projecting occiput or rear of the Neanderthal skull (this houses the large cerebellum and gives the long head) and the frontal "horns." The large eye sockets of the Neanderthal, altogether typical of nocturnal creatures (such as the owl), are better seen in figure 2.1.

And guess what—anthropologists refer to modern humans, ourselves, as hunter-gatherers! This is a rare but welcome nod in the direction of our duality—the duality that I, of course, insist on, and for which there is abundant evidence.

LEFT-HANDEDNESS

Let's now take a closer look at some of the aspects of left-handedness.

First, a comment on witches. They danced in circles—counterclockwise. As it happens, counterclockwise circling is the natural movement for a left-hander. Right-handers dancing in a circle move clockwise. Witches, of course, are closely associated with the moon and the night—and the devil. Once again, guess what? All medieval portraits of the magically raised devil show him stepping from the magic circle with his left hand outstretched. Well, well, well.

(And need I remind you that a witches' coven consisted of thirteen individuals?)

Let's now look at a rather different item.

All of us have noticed how difficult and awkward it is for a left-handed individual to use normal Western handwriting, which crosses the page from left to right.

But in five major languages/civilizations, namely in Chinese, Japanese, Hebrew, Arabic, and the ancient Egyptian hieroglyphs, writing crosses from *right* to *left*—which is of course the natural direction/movement for a left-hander.

Go on, pick up a Japanese book today. The back cover is the front cover! The first page is the last page. It's all back to front—as far as we right-handers are concerned. (I only realized this myself when one of my books was translated into Japanese!)

So, sir/madam, how did that Chinese, Hebrew, Japanese, and so forth, situation arise—that is, handwriting from right to left, in a world that is very predominantly right-handed—and in which *actual* left-handedness is hated, despised, and punished, as we shall soon see, throughout *all* history and *all* cultures worldwide? I reiterate, why should handwriting in major modern cultures today be so difficult and awkward for the very large majority of the actual population?

Has this situation never struck you as odd, weird, sir/madam? Have you any explanation? (No, of course you haven't.)

I do not myself have a *provable* answer to this riddle. But there is certainly a very likely explanation. This is that left-handed Neanderthals had already, in fact, produced the first form of handwriting—not necessarily letters as such, but stylized shapes, patterns, hieroglyphs—which, nevertheless, recorded events, conveyed instructions, messages, and whatever, just like the Egyptian hieroglyphs—at the time when Neanderthals and Cro-Magnons first met up. The Cro-Magnons at that point had not discovered or invented writing, and so took over the idea from the Neanderthals in the form (right to left) the Neanderthals had produced it.

If the idea of Neanderthals producing a form of handwriting sounds wild, we *do* have a very clear indication that Neanderthals could use rows of stones set out on the ground as an abacus to calculate, for instance, the star cycles, the periodicity of planets, and whatever—because the Tamils did *precisely* this in early historical times. And, of course, our present abacus appears among the Chinese, the Japanese, the Incas, and elsewhere—yet *another* example of so many parallel cultural phenomena found worldwide (which could only have come from one once-central source).

But let's just emphasize the main point in question once again. Hebrew, Arabic, old Egyptian, Chinese, and Japanese writing is from right to left. And, as it happens, these ethnic groups (among others) have clearly more physical Neanderthal characteristics than those shown by Europeans—for instance, the sloping forehead, the prognathous mouth, the recessive chin, the short height, and so on.

We turn now to etymology.

In all languages of the world, the word for "right" produces a host of positive derivatives. But the word for "left" produces none. Moreover, the word for "left" itself means something very derogatory and is further vilified in a series of derogatory epithets.

So in English, derived from the same root as the word *right,* we have: correct, direct, rectitude, erect, erection, rector, rectify, regal, royal, regime, regiment, forthright, upright, rights, and so forth. Also from the Greek word for right, *deks,* we get (never mind what they get) dexterous, dignify, decent, decree, doctrine, decorum, and others. From the French *droit* we get adroit. And so on.

But as already noted, the root for *left* (with its, in any case, negative meaning) produces *no derivatives whatsoever.* Instead, we have a host of contemptuous epithets: cack-handed (which, in British slang, means "shit-handed"), squiffy, wacky, bollock-handed, molly-handed (that's "soft-handed"), coochy, southpaw, cowpaw, and so on.

Actual left (*lyft*) in Anglo-Saxon means weak, worthless, womanish. Italian *mancino* means dubious and dishonest. Latin *sinister* means the same as our own word *sinister.* French *gauche* means awkward. In Indonesia, left means ignorant and foolish. Japanese *hiddarimaki* means mad. In various African languages, left means hated/unclean and weak/stupid, among others. And so on *throughout the whole world.* (You don't mind me saying that again, sir/madam? Throughout the whole world.)

May we mention in passing that Islam specifically states that Muslims must use their left hand to wipe their bums and for all other unclean purposes, and the right for all honorable purposes?

Left-handedness itself was (we should say is—see below) also actually *punished* and persecuted, throughout the whole world. In many tribes the left hand of a left-handed child was tied to the body—and sometimes actually mutilated—to prevent its use.

Incredibly, but in fact (and *why* is this so, sir/madam, why?), the Chinese and Japanese *today* report zero left-handedness in their populations.

All their left-handers are still "corrected" (that is, "righted"). But luckily for me, in 1976 E. L. Teng and colleagues conducted a survey in which they asked adult Chinese whether they remembered being "corrected" in their early life. And 18 percent reported yes. And these same individuals—just to emphasize that no *fantasy* is involved here—*still* used their left hand for minor and not readily noticed tasks.

So actual left-handedness in China is in fact *double* that reported in Europe! And just in case you think that Europeans can reprimand or criticize Asians, Italy—yes, Italy—still today also reports zero left-handedness. Incredible but true.

And we have no cause for smugness in Britain either. In 1937, a survey reported 5.8 percent left-handedness among males. In 1959 the figure reported had increased to 6.7 percent. In 1976 the figure had again increased to 11.3 percent . . .

We have to ask again (and again and again and again)—where has this *universal* loathing, hatred, and fear of left-handedness come from? Orthodoxy, of course, has *no answer whatsoever* to this question.

(And in case you are wondering—are left-handers in some way underachievers or pathetic in any sense?—here are just a few names of *actual* left-handers: Beethoven, Michelangelo, Leonardo da Vinci, Goethe, Nietzsche, Holbein, Landseer, Cicero, Tiberius, Lewis Carroll, Charlie Chaplin, Judy Garland, Paul McCartney, Cole Porter, Danny Kaye, John MacEnroe, Jimmy Connors, Pele, Babe Ruth, and many others.)

Here we must make a very, very important point. There is no question whatsoever of any kind of *instinctive* or *biological* reaction on our part to left-handedness. *None whatsoe*ver.

You can test this matter easily for yourself. While waiting in a post office or bank with a friend, ask your friend casually: "Was that chap who wrote the check/that cashier that served us/that woman ticking her shopping list/whatever left-handed or right-handed?" Or better still, while watching television: "That gunman who just shot the policeman—was he left-handed or right-handed?" You will get a blank, puzzled look from your friend: "I don't know."

So let me ask you personally. You've seen the individuals concerned many, many times on television. So the question is: Is former president Bill Clinton left-handed or right-handed? Was President Reagan left-handed or right-handed? Is former president George H. W. Bush (George W. Bush's father) left-handed or right-handed?

You don't know. In fact, all three are/were left-handed.

The treatment of left-handers and the attitudes toward left-handedness we are examining are not in any way instinctive—they are purely and totally sociopolitical.

We have already mentioned that witches danced counterclockwise and that circling counterclockwise is the natural movement for a left-hander—right-handed people circle clockwise. Now, guess what? Viewed from any point north of the equator, the sun (rising in the east, setting in the west) circles the Earth clockwise. The moon rising in the west and setting in the east circles the Earth counterclockwise. (So the moon is left-handed.)

These facts are recorded in the symbol of the swastika—which is, by the way, found *worldwide* in all cultures. Shall we say that again? The symbol of the swastika is found *worldwide*.

First, let us remember that the cross symbolizes the moon (worldwide). These "four arms of the moon," as many tribes actually call them, are derived from the four quarters of the moon. The cross is often shown enclosed in a circle (the moon itself, of course). Now, if we make small breaks in that circle at appropriate points, we produce the cursive (running) swastika—the swastika with bent arms as opposed to straight arms. And, in fact, we get *two* cursive swastikas: the swastika that runs to the left (the *sauvastika*) and the swastika that runs to the right (the *svastika*—see figure 2.3). These, of course, represent the actual movements of the two heavenly bodies. (We note in passing that it was the right-moving clockwise *svastika* the Nazis adopted for their symbol.)

Incredible how all the many items we are looking at hang together, isn't it?

There is yet another very, very important aspect to left-handedness.

Figure 2.3. Progressive development of the moon symbol (cross within a circle) into the cursive sauvastika and svastika, and thence into the conventional modern swastika (left- and right-facing varieties).

In all cultures *worldwide* and *throughout history* (yet again!) the left is associated with the feminine.

Thus in Africa, males are buried lying on their right side, the females lying on their left side. In India, the god Siva is male on the right side, female on the left. In classical Greece, left is stated as female, right as male—and specifically the left testicle is said to produce female children, the right testicle male children. The Maoris of New Zealand also state that the right hand is male, the left is female. And so on and so on.

This item is, of course, still on full view among ourselves today. For example, women button their coats to the left, men button theirs to the right. And, as already stated, our word *left* actually means weak, worthless, womanish.

And *yet*—and *yet*—in *all* ethnic groups through out the world today, there are *fewer* left-handed females than males. Shall we repeat that? *In all ethnic groups today, there are fewer left-handed females than males.*

So in the British surveys quoted earlier, the respective figures for the incidence of left-handedness among males and females were: 5.8 percent male, 3.7 percent female; 6.7 percent male, 4.4 percent female; 11.3 percent male, 8.8 percent female.

We have—that is, our search for the truth has—been very, very lucky here. For if there were more left-handed females in all (or indeed in any) ethnic groups, there would have been no point whatsoever for us—for me—to make.

But *in fact,* as stated, there are fewer left-handed females than males in every single ethnic group. And yet every single culture worldwide, both past and present, states that left is female and right is male.

My own explanation, of course, is that Neanderthal humans were left-handed and that their society was ruled and led by women. And so we are dealing with a memory of—and a reaction to—that situation, as in so many, many other cases.

But, specifically, why should there be fewer left-handed women than men in the world today? My own explanation is based on the persecution of witchcraft—our direct "modern" descendant of the ancient Neanderthal moon religion.

Estimates of the number of women burned or executed as witches in the last few thousand years in Europe alone run into millions. The highest estimate I have seen is 9 million. But even more cautious estimates suggest 3 or 4 million. These figures are absolutely staggering given, for example, that the total population of Britain in Shakespeare's time was only 2 million.

It seems quite clear, at any rate, that the number of women executed as witches is *huge.* This is during the last few thousand years in Europe alone. But I, of course, maintain that this persecution has been going on for the last 35,000 years—since Cro-Magnon first met up with Neanderthal. Now, if all or most of the women executed were left-handed—and were not over childbearing age—then the left-handed female gene was effectively being removed from the overall gene pool.

We witness this effect perfectly clearly when, for instance, we kill all the curly-haired pups in a dog population for generation after generation. Eventually curly-haired pups cease to be born at all. This is precisely how animal and plant breeders produce the qualities they want and remove the qualities they do not want from any genus of animal or plant.

The main target of the witch-hunters was women—but, of course, left-handed males (or wizards) would also have suffered—so female left-handedness in particular, but also left-handedness in general, would have been significantly reduced and held in check.

But, as we shall see, it is a very different story with regard to *other* Neanderthal genes in our pool. As I will argue in detail later, these have been steadily on the increase over the last 30,000-odd years.

One more item here on left-handedness.

A remarkable fact is that the language of the Basque people of northern Spain and southern France is not related to any other language of the world. It is one of the only languages in the world not related to others. One or two commentators have suggested that Basque may be the descendant of an actual Neanderthal language.

But the still more remarkable *fact* for me is that the Spanish take *their* word for "left" from the Basque word for "left"!

So is it the case that there is a much higher incidence of left-handedness among Basques? No data available. Are there significant numbers of redheads among Basques? No data available. A very tantalizing situation.

(So students, if any of you are looking for a research project . . .)

Chapter 3

Our Denial
of Menstruation

WE HAVE ALREADY DEALT with the rejection and punishment of left-handedness worldwide and throughout history.

But there is another far more dramatic—far, far more dramatic—situation found once again, as ever, worldwide and throughout all cultures and history, that being the reaction to menstruation.

The material involved would fill a whole book (has filled whole books, such as Shuttle and Redgrove's *The Wise Wound*). So just a sample here. But before we get to these items, let us stress that menstruation and moon are absolutely one and the same item. (Robert Briffault, in his 1927 book, *The Mothers,* writes: "All peoples of the world refer to menstruation as the moon.") Among Africans, Australian Aborigines, Asian Indians, and others, moon and menstruation are the very same word (also, of course, in our own menstruation and moon).

First, among American Indians in recent times: Any living thing that a menstruating woman touches with her foot will die. If a man walks where a menstruating woman has walked, his legs will swell up. If a man touches an object touched by a menstruating woman, he will become ill. Any spear, arrow, or other weapon touched by a menstruating woman becomes useless. The menstruating woman must live apart from the rest of the tribe in a special hut for four or five days (seven to eight days in Central America). A menstruating woman must drink water through a hollow bone. If she touches water directly or goes near any lake or stream, the fish will fail. (Eskimos and Lapps also have precisely the same view.) In some tribes, any menstruating woman breaking the many strict rules applied to her was put to death. Put to death!

In Africa, a look from a menstruating woman would either turn a man to stone or into a talking tree. If a menstruating woman touches her husband's weapons, he will be killed in his next battle. If she drinks milk, the cattle will die. If a male eats food touched by a menstruating woman, he will lose his virility and become ill. If she sleeps in his bed or sits in his chair, he will die. If she approaches a spring or a well, the water supply will cease.

Australia, again in recent times: A menstruating woman must not eat fish or go anywhere near water, otherwise the fish supply will fail. If she harvests food, the food supply will fail. Anyone eating food touched by a menstruating woman becomes ill. If a boy sees menstrual blood, he becomes an old man and turns gray. If a menstruating woman walks on a path used by males, or touches a possession of any male, she is put to death. (You hear that? Put to death.)

Jews: if a menstruating woman walks between two men, one of them will die. (The Jewish Sector, Tohoroth 1, the Book of Cleanness, devotes 509 pages to the taboos and observances concerning menstruation!) Arabs: the shadow of a menstruating woman causes crops and plants to die. Hindus: a man who goes near a menstruating woman loses his eyesight, knowledge, physical strength, and sexual virility. In Europe—yes, Europe—the presence or touch of a menstruating woman causes crops and plants to die; wine to turn to vinegar; milk to turn sour; well water to become contaminated; bees to die; mares to miscarry; and on and on.

The foregoing, then, is but a tiny sample of the detail involved. But we can add and stress that people and cultures all over the world excluded the menstruating woman—she had to live in a special hut or tent or room often well away from the main camp, had to wear a hood, had to be fed by other women using tubes or spoons, could not use paths, was isolated in every way and sense.

Well, well, well—how on earth did all that mad stuff come about, *worldwide,* sir/madam? (In reality, of course, the menstruating woman produces *none* of these effects whatsoever.)

We must also stress here the many obvious *parallels* in all cultures—such as causing plants and animals to die, causing a male to lose his virility, not being allowed to touch food. In this last connection, we have not mentioned that a menstruating woman is not allowed to touch salt or have salt in her own food.

As ever, we ask, could these many parallels have arisen by chance or coincidence? No, they are yet further proof of a once-shared central source of all the material contained in this book.

So is that it concerning menstruation? No way! Now we can look at the treatment of a girl at her *first* menstruation. You will scarcely believe some of these items—but they are all attested to by numerous clergymen, missionaries, and explorers in recent times.

First, various tribes in Africa.

In the Loango tribes, a girl having her first menstruation—a pubescent girl—is confined to a hut. She must not be seen by men. Her head must be covered with a blanket, because if the sun's rays were to touch her, she would become a living skeleton. She must stay in the hut for a fortnight. Neither she nor the girls who attend her may drink milk, or the cattle will die.

Among the Bagavda, the pubescent girl must not touch food; she is fed by other girls. In (former) Tanganyika, the pubescent girl is secluded for at least a month. She must not see the sun nor touch the ground. She must wear a collar of thorns, live in darkness, and eat poor food. Among the Waiomi, the pubescent girl must live in a secluded house for a year (!). She must not herself touch food and is fed by other females. She must not be spoken to; she must communicate only by signs. (And that's for a whole year.)

Elsewhere in Africa: any man who looks at a pubescent girl will be struck blind. She must not have milk. Any objects touched by her must be subsequently buried in a secret place. During two or three months' seclusion, her hair is shaved off, and she is smeared every day with red dye. If these or other ceremonies are not performed, she will either become barren or produce deformed children, rain will cease to fall, crops and hunting will fail. That's Africa.

But in Indonesia, New Guinea, and associated areas, in some tribes the pubescent girl is kept four or five years—that's *four or five years*—in a small cage of broad leaves sewn together. She has room only to sit or lie in a crouched position, is in continued darkness, and must not touch the ground. Several of these cages would be crammed into a house some twenty-five feet long and wide. She is allowed out of the cage once a day to bathe in a wooden dish outside the hut.

British New Guinea: The pubescent girl is kept for two or three *years* indoors in a raised house and is never allowed to descend to the ground; no sun is to enter the house. (In some tribes, the incarceration lasted only weeks or months.)

But in Borneo, a pubescent girl could be shut in a room in a house for as long as seven years (!) and never allowed to leave this room for any reason whatsoever. Body growth became stunted, skin pale and waxy, and so on. (In fact and of course, under such conditions, especially in the case of pubescent girls, although also sometimes for menstruating women, the individual concerned died—or became seriously ill—and acquired physical disabilities for life. The mind just boggles at this incredible situation. And yet why, sir/madam, do we/have we never heard in colleges and at universities anything of this situation and these practices?)

In the Torres straits, *only* three months' seclusion in a room, surrounded by bushes, is required. As ever, the pubescent girl may not touch food and must be fed only by other women. No man may see her.

In Australia, *only* four to six months' seclusion in a special hut is needed. But also during this period, the pubescent girl may occasionally be buried up to her hips in sand for several days. Other tribes cover the girl with sand or soil, then build a hut over her. Sometimes the girl would be severely weakened during the seclusion. As always, no sunlight must touch her, no man may see her.

There are various lengths of seclusion among North American Indians. The pubescent girl may not see the outside world or be touched by the sun; her head is often kept covered with a blanket; she must be fed by others; she may not have any animal food of any kind; any person touching her will die; she may be buried up to her armpits or chin in hot sand for a few days.

We should mention that sometimes the confined pubescent girl or menstruating woman would be carried twice a day to perform toilet functions. But in many cases, these functions had to be performed in the enclosed space—the conditions must have been quite appalling.

Queen Charlotte Islands: The pubescent girl was secluded for twenty days. Then during the next six months, she had to wear a cloak or hood of cedar bark reaching below her breasts. *She was allowed to eat only black cod for four years,* otherwise the fish population would disappear. She was not allowed to look at the sea or a fire for forty days. Not allowed to walk below the high-tide mark for a year, otherwise the tide would cease to be.

South American Indians: The pubescent girl was sewn in a hammock for two or three days, with just a small hole to breathe and no food. In other tribes, she was sewn into the hammock for a month with very little to eat, no animal food or fish whatsoever—that particular ban could last for a year.

Sometimes there were also ceremonies—for example, the pubescent girl was placed face down on a flat stone, then her back scarred with an animal tooth until the blood ran. Ashes were rubbed into the wounds; she was beaten with rods and then covered with biting ants; she was starved until she became a living skeleton.

Brazil. The pubescent girl is starved for a month in a secluded hut, then beaten by friends and relations till she falls senseless (or dead). But if and when she recovers, the beating is repeated four times at intervals of six hours.

Orinoco: She is sewn in a hammock and starved, then blindfolded and tied to a post. The old men of the tribe then whip her—the cords often carrying sharp spikes—until blood runs.

Cambodia: The pubescent girl must stay in bed under a curtain for up to 100 days. The general seclusion could last up to several years. During this time, she could not eat flesh or fish, only vegetables. She may not see sunlight in all this time.

Alaskan Eskimos: The pubescent girl was confined to a small hut *and made to remain on hands and knees for six months.* Then she was moved to a large hut where she *had to kneel with a straight back for a further six months.* She was allowed no social intercourse during all this time.

The incredible—but true—list is *unending,* but we will stop here. Similar practices would have undoubtedly also existed in Europe in early times, because we have traces of them in historical times—the menstruating woman or pubescent girl was fed with a long spoon.

Before considering how and why these worldwide practices came into being, we must first *emphatically* and unequivocally emphasize that males have no instinctive or inborn reaction or response whatsoever to menstruation. The responses we have listed are purely and totally sociopolitical (just as with left-handedness) and, specifically, religious.

Thus a man today (or tonight!) shares his bed with his menstruating wife without giving the matter a second thought, and, of course, without any kind of consequential effect whatsoever. Similarly, all of us (both males and females) sit next to menstruating women on trains and buses every day, stand next to them in supermarkets, and so on and so forth. There are, of course, no consequences whatsoever from this situation. Menstruating women also work in the garden. The plants don't notice! Also, menstruating women prepare food for their families—again, no ill effect whatsoever. Pubescent girls, forming part of a normal family as they do, also produce/cause no effects whatsoever. Well, there's no need nor point in continuing. We know that all the negative effects attributed to menstruating women worldwide are all, in objective terms, absolute rubbish. They are absolute rubbish.

And in reality, of course, menstruation is actually a positive phenomenon. It is evidence that a woman is fertile and can produce children. A pubescent girl's first menstruation is a signal that the girl is now able to become a mother and is about to turn into a curvy woman fancied by men. (Nothing wrong with that!)

So *absolutely and emphatically,* we do need an *explanation* for the horrendous (and of course *worldwide*) actions against menstruation and menstruating women that we have described. *How* could it all have arisen? How? How? How?

My own explanation is that the worship of menstruation was a central feature—and probably *the* central feature—of the Neanderthal moon religion. We have already pointed out that our word *Sabbath* is in fact the name of the monthly festival of the menstruation of the Moon Goddess. And, of course, we must not forget that I say Neanderthal culture—or civilization, as I will insist—was ruled and led by the females. I propose also that the moment of a girl reaching puberty and having her first menstruation was in that religion a very special ceremony (and I further suggest that the Orthodox Jewish bar mitzvah ceremony of a boy reaching manhood at age thirteen—did I say thirteen?—when, of course, he is 13 × 13 lunar months old is, in fact, a clear echo of that Neanderthal practice).

We will get to further detail of the Neanderthal moon religion in due course, along with the point that the extreme fear and loathing that Neanderthals as a whole produced in Cro-Magnons was not just fear of the Neanderthals as such, but of their moon religion in particular, which had to be punished and destroyed.

RED OCHRE

This is probably a good moment to look at red ochre.

My own proposal is that for Neanderthals, red ochre represented the menstrual blood that covered the Earth when the moon gave birth to her. Moon, Earth, and sun represent Mother, Daughter (yes, daughter), and Father. And *that,* I propose, is the origin of the Christian Holy Trinity—Father, Son, and Holy Ghost—the idea of the trinity itself being retained, but, of course, totally masculinized. (Never mind, daughter, there isn't even a mother in our Holy Trinity!)

First, here are the words of Adrian Boshier and Peter Beaumont on red ochre:

> Investigation of Palaeolithic, Mesolithic and Neolithic tombs throughout the world in every climate and continent reveal striking similarities in the funerary habits of man. Of all their affinities none are more commonly encountered than the custom of including red pigment with the buried body. This took the form of lumps of red stone scattered about the grave or the liberal coating of the deceased with the ground powder of a red mineral substance (red ochre). In some cases the dead were completely submerged in a mass of red ochre. So numerous are the references to their ochre internments that pages could be filled by quoting their provenance.

So there we are again—*striking* similarities in all cultures throughout the whole world and throughout all history.

In South Africa, there is clear evidence of the mining of red ochre throughout the last 100,000 years. The mining involved a significant use of manpower. At one site alone, half a million stone digging tools have been found, all showing considerable wear.

(A relevant and interesting point is that these mines were painstakingly refilled after excavation had been completed—this, the Swazi say, was to placate the Great Plumed Serpent. Here is a clear reference to the snake—which is also the dragon, as we shall see—that represents the moon in all cultures worldwide, along with the spider.)

On the worldwide aspect—we have an 80,000-year-old burial in red ochre of a boy in the Lebombo Mountains of South Africa. In southern France, the burial of a man 45,000 years ago, packed in red ochre. In Wales, dated between 35,000 and 25,000 years old, the Red Lady of Paviland, a woman buried in a large amount of ochre. At Lake Mugo in Australia, 30,000 years ago, the burial of a man sprinkled with red ochre. In Czechoslovakia, 23,000 BP, the Fox Lady, heavily covered with red ochre.

So many, many burials worldwide throughout all history in red ochre.

Then we have the use of red ochre by the living—we used to call the natives of North America Red Indians precisely because they ritualistically rubbed their bodies and hair with red ochre. So did the natives of Africa. So did the Aborigines of Australia. And so on and so on. We can also specifically mention that carved bones showing phases and cycles of the moon were worldwide rubbed with red ochre.

John Greenway asks,

Why did this material in almost every religion since Neanderthal man invented this institution become the most spiritually rich and magical of all substances—there is no end to the myriad uses of red ochre!

Raymond Dart comments,

Red ochre has a fantastic cultural evolutionary history beginning with prehistoric burial ritual and extending through its manifold late Palaeolithic artistic, religious, trading and bartering applications. By means of its dominating agency in the diffusion of the myths, rites and mysteries of ancient metallurgy and alchemy, it has played parts of such continuity and expanding diversity as to have rendered it unique amongst all minerals in moulding mankind's existence then and today.

(A point well worth mentioning is that in Australia *today,* there is a very powerful Aboriginal secret society called the Red Ochre Men. This society, about which very little is known, operates throughout the whole of Australia and *puts to death* any Aborigine violating the laws and commands of ancient religious myths.)

My own view, as already stated, is that for the Neanderthals, red ochre represented the placental blood that covered the Earth when the moon gave birth to her (as well as, certainly, the blood of menstruation itself). Covering a corpse with placental blood at burial ensured the rebirth of the individual in the next life, or afterlife. (No commentator, incidentally, disputes that red ochre represents blood of some kind.)

What we must emphasize very, very strongly is that red ochre is of no practical use whatsoever. Its value is *purely* symbolic and ritualistic—and so, of course, we do need a very powerful explanation for its importance worldwide, and in particular, its centrality in Neanderthal religion and culture.

What the Neanderthals certainly knew—had learned during their endless mining of the substance—is that red ochre is decayed and metamorphosed magnetite (also known as lodestone or "leading stone"). And that a sliver of magnetite floating in water (water being a very important moon element, as we shall see) points to the North Pole.

Yet another of my "convenient fantasies"? No way. For the American Indians 3,000 years ago used slivers of magnetite on a piece of wood floating on water as a compass. As did also the Chinese 2,000 years ago. So the American Indians were well ahead of the *alleged* discovery of the compass by the Chinese! But, of course, the American Indians themselves had probably emerged from China 20,000 or more years ago, crossing into America. So we are quite certainly talking of a very ancient common practice.

The North Pole itself is very important, because this is the still center of the heavens around which the starry universe revolves. And I suggest that the Neanderthals saw the heavens as a giant spider's web, with the North Pole at its center. This is one of the reasons why the spider (along with the snake) was central to the moon religion and why once again (again! again!) *worldwide and throughout history,* both the spider and the snake are identified with, and in fact actually represent, the moon. We'll get more on that in due course.

First, some other matters.

Chapter 4
All Fairy Tales Are True

BEFORE GETTING INTO FURTHER detail on Neanderthal society and culture, let's consider—and explain—some important items that are otherwise unexplainable (like so much of what we've already seen)—and, of course, are *not* explained or even considered by our totally inadequate academics.

As we know, Neanderthals had strong, projecting bone eyebrow ridges and a flattened, receding forehead. These are facts. I myself consider that Neanderthals had strong projecting eyebrows which further extended the bony projections. (You can see these individuals around you today—there's a British Labour politician who is quite a good example.) But there is, in fact, no need for any kind of speculation, because we have ample proof of this from the many sightings or *actual captures* of "wild men" (see below).

The flattened forehead and the projecting brow bones (further augmented by the projecting eyebrows), of course, strongly resemble the horns and flattened forehead of, for example, goats, deer, and other horned creatures. I further propose that when a Neanderthal attacked, he lowered his head, then ran and butted his opponent.

Convenient fantasy number 2,708 on my part? Again, as ever, no way. Because Eskimos to this day settle their quarrels by lowering their heads, charging, and butting each other until one submits! What a coincidence.

So this, I say, is why the Christian devil has horns (and cloven feet). I claim the Christian devil is a memory of actual Neanderthals. An actual memory of actual Neanderthals.

Then we have the Great God Pan. He has horns, is hairy, and has cloven hooves. He plays a set of pipes—the pipes of Pan. And guess what? *Guess what?* A recent discovery is that of a Neanderthal bone flute that is 82,000 years old. So Neanderthals actually played the flute! It is clear, therefore, that Pan is also, once again, a memory of actual Neanderthal man.

(Involved too in this general context is the "horned moon"—for example, Freija is the "horned goddess" who is also the moon. In fact, all moon gods and goddesses are bulls and cows. And then we have the Minotaur—the creature with the body of a man and the head of a bull, who lives at the center of the Cretan labyrinth—which, as we shall see, is a moon temple. The Minotaur is, I claim once again, the Neanderthal.)

Another of my arguments is that when a Neanderthal submitted in combat, he turned and presented his buttocks, just as chimpanzees do. Again, no fantasy whatsoever on my part is involved here, because, in historical times, Africans submitted in battle by turning and presenting their buttocks! Yes, they did.

And so *this* is why satanists and devil worshippers present their buttocks to the altar. That was why the Neanderthals did. (It is, of course, what chimpanzees would do if they moved up the evolutionary scale.) (But Europeans—that is, Cro-Magnons—submit in battle by lowering their heads and kneeling, and so this is what Christians do when *they* go to the altar and pray.)

We can now make a very important point here. Every scrap of superstition, every fairy tale, old wives' tale, every "fanciful" legend derives from some once *real* and *actual* situation. The material in question does *not* come out of thin air from nowhere. Yes, the items become garbled over the course of time—and their point of origin gets totally forgotten. But none of this is fantasy.

Thus, for example, gnomes, goblins, and elves said to live deep in forests are memories of Neanderthals. (And as we shall conclusively see, *actual* Neanderthals at this very moment in time—that is, now, *today*—still survive and live at the edges of our civilization, as Myra Shackley has described in detail in her book *Still Living? Yeti, Sasquatch and the Neanderthal Enigma*.) Thus fairies are principally female because (magical) Neanderthal society was led by women. And the devil is left-handed because Neanderthal was left-handed—as I claim, but some proof of Neanderthals' left-handedness follows shortly. (And, of course, there's that Siberian tribe already mentioned, 66 percent of whom are left-handed.)

Gnomes and elves are shown and described as having large pointed ears. So did Neanderthals have large pointed ears? I certainly say yes. You can see these in occasional individuals today (as Oswald Spengler remarked, "You can observe Neanderthal at any public gathering"). But also, and absolutely crucially, drawings (and descriptions) of wild men portray them having pointed ears! Figure 4.1 on page 34 shows (a) an item from a Carthaginian bowl depicting an attack on an outlying town and (b) a Mongolian wild man from an eighteenth-century Tibetan manuscript.

Both these wild men have pointed ears. Both are also completely covered with body hair. And both are using their *left* hands!

In fact, *all* drawings and carvings of wild men that I have ever seen showing them doing something *show them using their left hand*. Well, lucky, lucky me.

The pointed "animal" ears of Neanderthals, of course, further increased the Cro-Magnons' perception of them as bulls/deer/goats. So, to repeat this once again, none of our "fantasies" about mythical creatures are fantasies. They are facts.

In general, then, our ancient history (both cultural and evolutionary) is remembered and recounted (in legends, fairy stories, and so on) without any realization that the material *is* actually real and is *in fact* ancient history. But also, sometimes there are individuals and groups—

Figure 4.1 (a) Wild man using left hand to throw an object, Carthaginian bowl design (seventh century BC). (b) Mongolian wild man with left hand raised (eighteenth-century Tibetan manuscript).

that is, secret societies—in which there is some actual preserved memory of the real origins of the material, and certainly belief that it is true. These individuals and societies sometimes knowingly and deliberately insert the items concerned into *current* practices and organizations. The Knights Templar, whom we have already mentioned, are an example of this gnostic preservation of ancient material and practice—and there is more to say on that with reference to the Order of the Garter itself. The Holy Grail is another deliberate and gnostic insertion of ancient material into our current beliefs, as we shall be discussing.

And absolutely clearly, the founders of the Christian religion were determined to preserve in it major detail of the ancient moon religion—as we have already seen, but still more to come on that score too.

Time now for a closer look at the wild man (and red hair).

How did I arrive at my view that Neanderthals had red hair long before the Oxford Institute for Molecular Biology did?

There were various suggestive leads. For example, the very large majority of individuals sacrificed in bog rituals and other ceremonies to ensure the fertility of crops or whatever, throughout Europe and the Middle East and during the last few thousand years, were redheads. (The dead individuals in the bog sacrifices were then buried in the bogs, which is why we have their actual remains.)

And incidentally, the redheads sacrificed in Egypt were said to represent Typhoon, who was the enemy of Osiris the Sun God. And the Neanderthals, and their religion, were indeed enemies of the sun, certainly in Cro-Magnon eyes.

Then, there are many unfavorable superstitions concerning redheads. For example, in Scotland and Ireland, it is said that if you meet a red-haired woman on your way to work, you should turn around and go home.

But quite conclusive evidence arises from the *actual capture* and descriptions of wild men.

A very, very striking and important example is the case of the wild woman Zana. She was captured in the Caucasus in the second half of the nineteenth century. She then lived freely among the villagers of Tkhina on the Moki River. She was totally covered in red body hair—!!—had a muzzle-like prognathous jaw, *large eyebrows,* and big white teeth. She produced four children by normal human fathers. Professor Boris Porshnev interviewed two of Zana's grandchildren in 1964. He described them as of somewhat Negroid appearance with very pronounced jaw muscles and jaws. They reported that their aunt, Zana's daughter, too, had extensive body hair. (So *women* covered all over with body hair!)

(Now, *why* haven't our scientists and academics queued up to examine the DNA of these individuals?) (Shouldn't they all be sacked?—*yes.*)

Let's look at another actual capture of a wild man in 1925, who was shot by Major General Mikhail Topilski and his men in Russia. Topilski writes (my italics):

At first glance I thought the body was that of an ape. *It was covered with hair all over.* The eyes were dark and the teeth were large and even and shaped like human teeth. *The forehead was slanting and the eyebrows were very powerful.* The protruding jaw bones made the face resemble the Mongol type of face. *The nose was flat with a deeply sunk bridge. The ears looked a little more pointed than a human being's.* The lower jaw was very massive. The feet much wider and shorter than man's.

But even more striking—for reasons that follow—is the description of a captured wild youth in Germany in 1784 by an anthropologist Michael Wagner (again, my italics):

His forehead was strongly bent inwards. He had heavy brown eyebrows which projected far out over his eyes. His mouth stood out somewhat. The back and chest were very hairy, the muscles on his legs were stronger and more visible than in ordinary people. He walked erect but a little heavily. It seemed as if he would throw himself from one foot to the other. He carried his head and his chest forward.

The projecting eyebrows are absolutely brilliant, aren't they? (Lucky me!)

We have very clear indications of Neanderthal here—the strongly backward-sloping forehead, obviously. Also, the walk is what the physical structure of the Neanderthal leads us to expect—the massive pyknic body type, the broad feet, and so forth.

But the absolutely and really, really, really crucial point to make here is this: *Michael Wagner had never even heard of the Neanderthals.* Nor had anyone else. The first Neanderthal fossil was discovered in 1856.

That's 1856. Seventy-two years after Wagner's description.

Many reliably reported *sightings* of wild men specifically mention red hair. So we have: thick reddish hair on the body, hair predominantly reddish brown, reddish-gray hair all over, brown to reddish hair, reddish-black hair, covered with reddish hair, and so on. Here is a detailed report of a sighting in 1970 by Mongolian peasants: "Half man and half beast with reddish hair. The back of the head had a conical shape, the forehead was flattened, prominent brow ridges and a protruding jaw." (Smart of these peasants to have read up on the precise details of the Neanderthal skull!)

Red is the hair color stated in the large majority of reports.

And often it is said (as we have already seen) that the whole body, arms, and legs are covered with hair (and such was the case, as we have already observed, with Zana, Topilski's wild man, and Wagner's wild boy). In this respect, we can look at the three sculptures shown in figure 4.2 on the following page.

All, of course, clearly drawn from life. All three are completely covered with hair—as are the other two wild men shown in figure 4.1. (Now can we understand that the wild man/Neanderthal is also the "mythical" werewolf—the man-wolf? We'll get around to zombies, vampires, and so on later.)

A very important item in the Devon figure is the missing front tooth in an otherwise perfect set of teeth. Clearly this is a very *deliberate* omission—and must have importance and significance.

It is actually evidence that Neanderthals ritually removed the front upper tooth. Or rather, I should say, *further* evidence, because, in fact, we have actual Neanderthal skulls from Israel, Gibraltar, and elsewhere in which one or both front upper incisors have been deliberately removed.

And guess what? *Guess what?* Australian Aborigine boys, at this present day, have one or both upper front incisors removed during their initiation ceremony into manhood. Well, well, well. How could these two common practices—among (a) Neanderthals and (b) Australian Aborigines—be any kind of *coincidence*? What are the chances of *that*?

And, of course, the missing tooth in the Devon portrait is *equally* proof of that picture's authenticity. It is a portrait of an actual surviving Neanderthal. (And that's in *Britain* in *historical times*.)

Let's go back once again to red hair.

Figure 4.2. (a) Peasant and captured wild man from thirteenth-century French church, Notre Dame, Semuris, Provence. (b) Stylized wild man from Devon, England, showing probable ritual removal of upper front incisor tooth. (c) Wild man carved on the exterior of Peasenhall Church in Suffolk, England, and clearly, as in 4.2a, drawn from life.

It will astonish most people to learn that red hair is quite common among the Australian Aborigines and the Maoris of New Zealand. (These came originally from southern India.) Among the many mummified bodies found in Peru, which are thousands of years old, the "great number" have red hair. The statues of Easter Island in the Pacific, which the inhabitants state are the "image of our ancestors," were crowned with a large red stone. This, say the islanders, was not a hat or a crown, but represented their hair. Red hair is quite common among

Jews—hence Danny "The Red" Cohn-Bendit—and in Poland there is a saying that all redheaded Poles are Jews. Red-haired individuals were also around in ancient Egypt—because it was they who were sacrificed in fertility rites. The Chinese (while not being redheaded themselves) have stories involving redheads. For example, Chinese alchemists consider the Philosopher's Stone to be red cinnabar and say that if this is mixed with honey and eaten, it restores youth, confers immortality, and turns your hair red.

So, *actual* redheads are/were found among Aborigines, Maoris, American Indians, Easter Islanders, Egyptians, Jews, and so forth. Is *that* not astonishing? And all cultures *worldwide,* in any case, have stories and legends concerning individuals with red hair.

(In medieval times in Europe, the aristocracy used to go hunting wild men in the forests. When the supply of wild men ran out, they turned to hunting *red* foxes—that's where fox hunting today comes from.)

All this red-haired stuff, and, of course, the actual redheadedness itself, *must* go back to European Neanderthals. What other explanation is there? None whatsoever. And, of course, we *do, do,* need an explanation. (Are you listening, academics and scientists?)

Then, as stated earlier in chapter 2, recent studies have shown that redheads are the most sexually active of all human groups. Well, well.

And we also have *proof* of the wild man's (that is, the Neanderthal's) rampant sexuality. The majority of wild men are, of course, red-haired . . . well, well, well.

So Albert Magnus, in the twelfth century, describes a wild man captured in Saxony. This wild man's "lack of reason," as Magnus puts it, was evidenced by his "ever trying to accost women and exhibit lustfulness."

And Michael Wagner's wild boy behaved thus: "As soon as he saw a woman he broke out into violent cries of joy, and tried to express his awakened desires through gestures."

An item I cannot resist inserting here concerns the Welsh people.

(It is amazing, is it not, how all the matters this book is considering hang together everywhere? And *that's* because it's all true!)

The rate of left-handedness in Wales is double that found in England. The Welsh are, on average, significantly shorter than the English. Red hair is very common in Wales. *The rate of marital infidelity among the Welsh is the highest in Great Britain.* The Welsh national symbol is the dragon (!). And there is an expression in English, "to welsh" (whose use is now banned, along with the verb "to jew"), which means to cheat and lie and break promises.

We'll get to that last item in detail later—but, of course, this is "Cro-Magnon" looking at "Neanderthal."

Chapter 5
Menstruation Was, in Fact, the First Religion

TIME TO LOOK AT the central ceremony of the Neanderthals' moon religion.

We already know that there was a monthly festival every twenty-eight days celebrating the menstruation of the moon goddess.

But the chief ceremony of the moon religion took place on the shortest day of the year (which, for us, is the 21st of December) and equally on the first day of their New Year (that's December 22 in our calendar).

On the shortest day the moon sacrificed the sun, the "King for a Year"—but then the next day graciously resurrected him so that life on earth could continue. (Does that sound anything like the death and resurrection of Christ? Of course it does.)

The Sun King was sacrificed by having his genitals removed to turn him into a menstruating woman. The blood was caught in a cup. This was then drunk and the genitals eaten, followed by the rest of the body.

And *that's* why Catholics today drink the blood and eat the body of Christ during Mass.

My view/explanation of this matter has good tangential support. A

Roman soldier thrusts a spear into the side of the sacrificed Christ (let's just remember again that the cross always symbolizes the moon). Joseph of Arimathea catches the blood in a cup. And that cup, of course, is the Christian Holy Grail.

There is a further significant item supporting my view. The king of the castle where the Grail is subsequently kept (Grail Castle), the Fisher King, is wounded by having a spear thrust through both thighs! Well, well, well—what a funny old wound. We are, *of course,* talking here of "the knife through both testicles." (And equally, the "spear in the side" of Christ is again a disguised reference to castration.)

I suggest also that the circumcision of males as practiced by Orthodox Jews, the removal of the male foreskin, is another echo of the central moon ceremony. We should stress that circumcision is (as ever!) practiced in many cultures worldwide—among Africans, American Indians, Australian Aborigines, and so forth. The Aboriginal ceremony of a boy reaching manhood is particularly dramatic—not just the foreskin is removed, but the penis is slit open end to end. When this is held up against the stomach, we have, of course, the vagina (a conclusion reached by Bruno Bettelheim, incidentally). The Aboriginal elders present eat portions of the foreskin and drink some of the blood. (They should have been Catholics!) Well, well, well.

In the main ceremony of the Moon Goddess, the sun is sacrificed on one day and resurrected the next, in midwinter. Christ, however, is sacrificed in the spring on one day, Friday, (which, however, just happens to be Freija's day) and is resurrected on the third day thereafter (Monday is Moon Day!). However, three is also a central moon number, as we have already seen—and there is more to come on that. And, of course, the date of Easter, in any case, is determined by the moon. We cannot say this too often. The date of the festival of the death and resurrection of Christ is determined by the moon.

The original birth of Christ is on December 25. This just happens to be three days away from the birth of the new sun on December 22. Did I say *three*? Coincidence?

No. There are, as we have seen, many moon references and circumstances in the story of Christ's birth, death, and resurrection—references in particular to the central yearly moon ceremony—far too many for any kind of coincidence to be involved.

This is probably a good point to state that the moon has three colors. These are white, red, and black.

During an eclipse of the moon, a coppery red fringe creeps across the full moon's face. The color is variable in intensity. "In some eclipses it is of a very deep red." So the moon does menstruate! And this situation, incidentally, is why the ceremony of the menstruation of the Moon Goddess (in Babylonia in historical times, for instance) takes place at the full moon and not at the new moon (when women menstruate).

But when an eclipse occurs after a volcanic eruption, we get what is known as a black lunar eclipse, "the moon is covered with a horrid black shield." Such an eclipse occurred in December 1964.

So this situation is why the Cow-Moon Goddess of the Ionians was said to change her color from white to red to black. And why the heifer calf born to Minos and Persephone changed its colors in the same way three (of course, three) times a day.

The three colors of the moon, are, I consider, also the origin of the *tricolor* flag that so many countries have.

We now get to detail of the Cretan maze.

CRETAN MAZE

The Cretan maze is another item—yet another—found in *all* cultures *worldwide* (see figure 5.1 on page 44).

How could such a maze be found and used (worshipped) everywhere, unless it came from *one* once *central* and powerful source? How could its existence worldwide be due to some coincidence or chance? (At least W. H. Matthews, writing in 1922, who unfortunately did not know then the *full* geography of the maze, wondered whether we

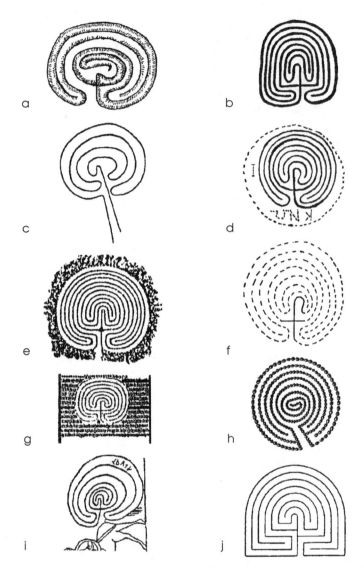

Figure 5.1. (a) North American Indian labyrinth, from an eighteenth-century Spanish manuscript. (b) Sacred symbol of the Hopi Indians. (c) Design from Nazca Plain, Peru. (d) Cretan labyrinth (coin design, Knossos). (e) Stone labyrinth from Gothland, northern Europe. (f) Rock carving, Cornwall, England. (g) Labyrinth from Rajasthan, India. (h) Stone labyrinth from Finland. (i) Etruscan vase representation of the Trojan "Troy Game." (j) A Welsh Caerdroia ("city of turnings"). All these items, separated not just by thousands upon thousands of miles, but tens of thousands of years, are quite obviously the same maze design.

were dealing with "a common origin of astounding antiquity." Yes, Mr. Matthews, we *are*.)

As we have already stated, at the center of the maze in Crete was said to live the Minotaur, the creature with the body of a man and the head of a bull (that is, a Neanderthal). The majority of Cretan mazes have seven inner circular paths. Seven is, of course, a central moon number, as we have seen.

The majority of these mazes also have a left-hand entrance. To enter a structure by a left-hand entrance is natural for a left-handed person. Recent studies have shown that if a large office block has two entrances adjacent to each other, one on the left hand and the other on the right, left-handed individuals will enter by the left door, right-handed people by the right door. So we have here pretty conclusive evidence that the original Cretan maze was designed by a left-hander.

(Actually the term *maze* is entirely incorrect. What we have here is a labyrinth. You get lost in a maze—you cannot get lost in a labyrinth. It has one way in and one way out. A labyrinth is a purely ritualistic item.)

My own view is that the Cretan maze was used, ritualistically, in the monthly ceremony of the menstruation of the Moon Goddess, as well as in the major yearly ceremony of the death and rebirth of the sun. I suggest that the maze is a stylized representation of the (female) human intestines and womb. And the rituals involved were, of course, fertility rituals.

Dancers carrying a cord—or linked by a cord—danced into and out of the labyrinth. So it was a continuous loop. This cord is quite certainly the umbilical cord of the newborn baby. I also consider that the garter worn by witches is a stylized version of the umbilical cord, and the cord of the maze. Witches wore this garter on the left leg, incidentally. (Brides in historical times also wore a garter, and threw it to the congregation after the wedding ceremony.) This is the source also of the Garter of the Knights of the Garter—another of their connections, then, with witchcraft, fertility, and the moon religion.

NEANDERTHAL CULTURE

We have clear *proof* that Neanderthals had an advanced culture—quite apart from much other reasonable speculation. So:

1. A recent discovery is that of a Neanderthal flute that is 82,000 years old. (So Neanderthals could compose music and play musical instruments—but nothing else?)

2. We have clear archaeological evidence from Iraq that Neanderthals (60,000 years ago) cared for the sick, the disabled, and the elderly. They also buried the dead in a mass of flowers and held a burial feast. The plants involved include many that were used medicinally in historical times: yarrow (which means "healer"), groundsel (which means "pus-swallower"), hollyhock (many uses against toothache, inflammation, spasms, and so on), and more.

3. We have the Drachenloch altar in Switzerland, already discussed, which is 75,000 years old. This is a chest built of stones, in a cave, and covered with a huge stone slab. In the chest itself are seven bear skulls with muzzles pointing toward the cave entrance. A further six skulls are in niches cut in the wall at the back of the cave (making a total of thirteen skulls).

4. From Hungary, we have clear evidence of a Neanderthal bear-pelt factory that is 50,000 years old.

5. A recent discovery in Spain is of Neanderthal blast furnaces—which are 53,000 years old! To quote a *Times* (London) article from 1996: ". . . blast furnaces to make tools . . . an astonishing variety of tools . . . proof that Neanderthal possessed a skill level far more advanced than he has so far been given credit for."

6. In Africa, as we have already seen, we have continuous and extensive mining of red ochre for a period of 100,000 years.

7. From Africa again, we have a stone carving of the Moon Goddess that is said to be 250,000 years old. (Yes—250,000 years.)

Now *how* could these items exist in an otherwise cultural vacuum? *How?* No way. These have to be *samples* from a vigorous, organized, and continuous culture.

Why, then, a critic might ask, do we not have *more* evidence from this enormous geographical area and very long time span—for example, of permanent physical structures?

One of the answers here is that I believe the Neanderthals considered permanent structures to be some kind of anathema or transgression.

Yet another of my "fantasies"? Again, as ever, no way.

For the Australian Aborigines to this day will spend weeks building a temple of rocks and trees—but as soon as the ceremony involved is finished, the temple is *completely* destroyed. So there you are. Another of my proposals, incidentally, is that the Neanderthals were basically nomadic—just like the gypsies and other groups—so no permanent dwelling sites or "towns."

The critic might also like to ask himself/herself this question. If the Australian Aborigines were suddenly wiped out, what trace would there be of their culture—of their elaborate religious ceremonies, and organizations like the Red Ochre men? Effectively none. Let us also mention here that the Aborigines, who have several hundred different languages, nevertheless have a universal sign language that enables all Aborigines to speak to each other—just as do the Indians of North America. But we would find no trace of this matter *archaeologically*.

(Incidentally, I myself consider that sign language was/is actually another Neanderthal invention—and that all Neanderthals could speak to each other. So there's a further project for you, students. Compare the Australian and American Indian sign languages. If there are strong similarities between the two, then we have yet another item pointing toward a once-common, ancient central source.)

Now, having said that we have no permanent physical structures (apart from the odd altar or blast furnace!), we come to the astonishing matter of the "Alaise" towns. We have to thank the Frenchman Xavier

Guichard and his book *Eleus Alesia*, published in 1936, for this material. No one else spotted this amazing situation.

Guichard showed that there are many, many hundreds of towns and villages throughout the whole of Europe and part of the Middle East, all with the same original name. That is a striking enough situation in itself. But absolutely amazingly, all these towns lie on twenty-eight (yes, twenty-eight) straight lines radiating from (that is, crossing through) the town of Alaise in France (see figures 5.2, 5.3, and 5.4).

All the sites/towns in question are of prehistoric origin. None date from historical times. All the towns are (a) on a hill by a river and (b) centered on a man-made water well.

Guichard himself considers that the sites were established by Indo-Europeans—but that, frankly, is rubbish. All the Indo-Europeans ever did was fight each other. In no way would they have cooperated in setting up such an arrangement—and in any case, why?

No, the sites were established either by the Cro-Magnons or the Neanderthals.

Now, the sites cluster most closely in the southwest. The Cro-Magnons entered Europe from the southeast (via the Middle East). Would we not expect sites to radiate from and cluster there? Also, the Cro-Magnons entering Europe had the major problems of dealing with the Neanderthals on the one hand, and with the sudden onset of a new ice age on the other. Hardly the circumstances in which to consider setting up a network of sites—and, in any case, *why*?

The case for considering the Neanderthals as the authors of the site network is very strong. Involved are twenty-eight straight lines—and that is a major moon number, as we know.

And what do the radiating straight lines remind us strongly of? A spider's web, obviously. We have already pointed out that the spider (along with the snake) is associated with the moon in all cultures worldwide and throughout history, though we have yet to consider why.

Could it be that the Neanderthals ritualistically circled through

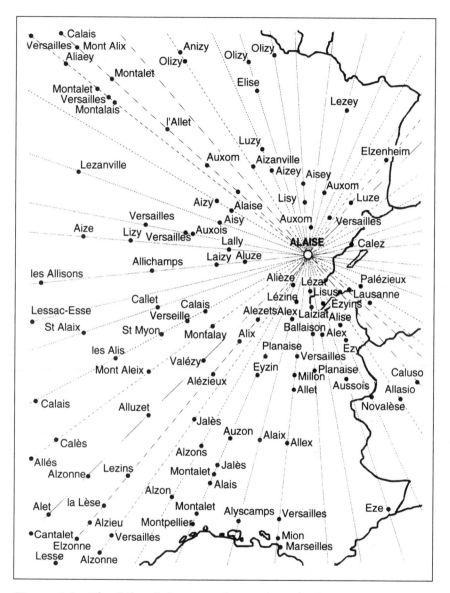

*Figure 5.2. The "Alaise" locations (towns having the same root name)
immediately surrounding the central town of Alaise itself (in France, Italy,
Switzerland, and Germany). Here, the locations cluster most thickly (just as,
perhaps, the spirals are densest at the center of the spider's web).*

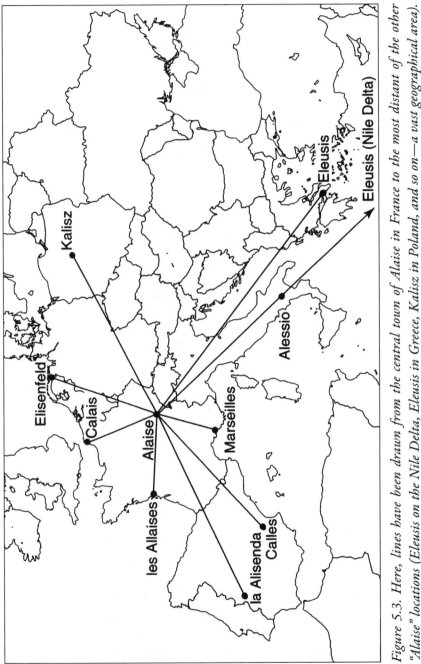

Figure 5.3. Here, lines have been drawn from the central town of Alaise in France to the most distant of the other "Alaise" locations (Eleusis on the Nile Delta, Eleusis in Greece, Kalisz in Poland, and so on—a vast geographical area). This is the hub of the Neanderthal empire, including Africa. (Does this structure not remind us very strikingly of the initial straight radials that the spider sets up before commencing the joining spirals?)

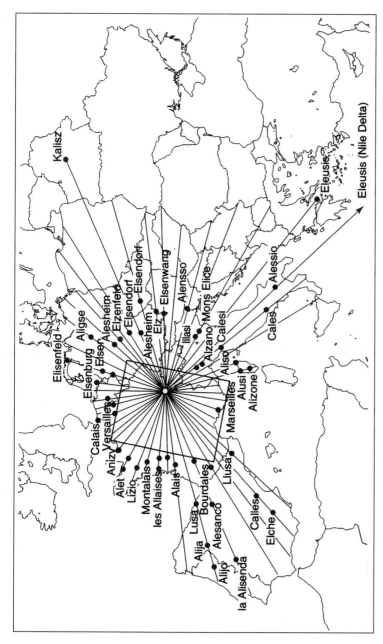

Figure 5.4. Here, twenty-four of the twenty-eight straight lines constructed by Guichard are shown, along which the very large majority of the "Alaise" locations are sited. Details of the rectangle at the center have already been indicated in figure 5.2. For reasons of space, by no means all of the Alaise towns are shown, either here or in the earlier illustrations. What possible explanation can orthodox thought offer for these many hundreds of identical names (in origin, that is) and for their precise layout over so many thousands of lateral miles and millions of square miles?

these sites, perhaps on a permanent basis—thus forming the rest of the spider's web? Or did youngsters on reaching womanhood/manhood have to perform this spiral journey ritualistically? Well, we do have the "walkabout" imposed on the Australian Aborigine boy when he reaches manhood, don't we?

Another item. Guess what—the Eleusis site in Greece—one of the terminal points of the radiating lines—has been famed for the last 5,000 years by reason of its, yes, orgiastic moon ceremonies!

There is more to consider. Alaise, the center of the web, is in eastern France. It was here that classic Neanderthals flourished. And it is also not far from where the Basques live today—who, among other things, as we know, *speak a language related to no other.* (As already stated, the Spanish take their word for "left" from the Basque word. And should we mention here another of the endless "coincidences" in the material we are studying? When the spider begins to make the spiral part of its web, it circles counterclockwise. The *spider* is *left-handed!*)

SPIDERS, SNAKES, AND DRAGONS

Time we looked a bit more clearly at these items.

As we have already said more than once, the spider and the snake are associated with the moon in *all* cultures *worldwide* and throughout history. And, as ever, we must ask ourselves the question: How could this situation arise except by these matters (and so many others) originating from some ancient once-central and very important source?

There is no other possibility here. For what is there about either the spider or the snake that could cause you or me or anyone else to associate either of them with the moon?

My own explanation is very simple. Neanderthal society was led and ruled by women (and worshipped the moon). Now, guess what? *The spider and the snake are the only two species on common view where the female is larger than the male.*

Shall I repeat that, sir/madam? The only two species on common view where the female is larger than the male.

How could Neanderthal women have resisted the temptation to put these two creatures at the top of their honors list?

Once the position of these two beings is established, we can then, of course, look around for associations. I have already suggested that Neanderthals might have considered the starry heavens to be a gigantic spider's web, centered on the North Pole. That view, of course, would be supportive for the spider.

What about snakes, then? Any further connection?

We know, as, of course, did the Neanderthals, that the moon controls the movement of tidal water. The moon (therefore) also controlled rain—which occurs, in any case, when the sun is absent. And if the sun does put in an appearance while rain is falling, then we get a rainbow, which can readily be considered to be a coiled snake. And *in fact,* the Australian Aborigines call this the Rainbow Serpent. And worship it centrally at the heart of their religion. They say it usually inhabits deep waters. Then again, the Mexican rain god, Tlaloc, is represented by two snakes twined together. There are dozens more such items we could mention. The rainbow-rain-snake connection is absolutely clear.

(And just incidentally, I would certainly say that Neanderthals considered that the moon also controlled the movement of glaciers, which are frozen water, and so caused ice ages to occur—these, then, of course, further subordinating the sun.)

During the rainstorms we get lightning—and now we get to the dragon.

All commentators agree that the dragon is a stylized snake. (The Greek word *draco* actually means snake.) And, as stated, the snake and rain are intimately connected.

So the forked lighting of a rainstorm is the forked tongue of the snake—and the forked tongue of the "dragon." And like the snake's bite, lightning also kills people. And again, the dragon is said to "breathe fire" because the rain-snake produces lightning—and again, of course, lightning very often does start actual fires. So that's the dragon sorted—well, almost.

There remains the question—how did/does the dragon acquire legs?

Well, you've seen the line of Chinese dancers celebrating the New Year who are covered with, are wearing, an artificial manufactured snakeskin. And guess what—African tribes also perform the "dancing snakes" routine. (Again, once again, clear evidence from two totally separated peoples of a common practice deriving from some once-central source.) Cro-Magnons, clearly, saw Neanderthals performing this ceremony (and others) and reported the matter. So that's how and why the mystical dragon, with legs, came into our culture.

And why do the Chinese today produce a snake to celebrate the beginning of New Year? I say it is because the snake is the moon, and the Moon graciously resurrects the dead Sun on New Year's Day.

THE PLEIADES AND THE GREAT BEAR

If the material involving the Pleiades were all that we (this book) had to show as evidence, it would be more, far more, than enough to smash our current orthodox view of history (the view broadcast in all our schools and universities) to pieces.

So, where to begin?

First, the Pleiades is a tiny and faint group of seven stars (yes, seven) that is very difficult to find and which has no characteristics that would cause it to be noticed (apart from seven, of course) by anybody. But here now is the legend of the Pleiades as told by the *ancient Greeks*.

Orion the hunter came across six sisters and their mother in a wood. Overcome with passion, he pursued the fleeing group through the forest for five years. At that point, Zeus took pity on the *seven* women and changed both the pursued and the pursuer into stars. So now in the sky we see the *seven* Pleiades females pursued by Orion the Hunter.

Here now is the story of the Pleiades as told by the *Australian Aborigines*.

Wurrunna the Hunter was out in search of game in a strange place. He came upon a camp, in which there were only seven young girls. The girls said they had come from a distant country, just out of curiosity, and were alone. Wurrunna decided this was a good chance to get himself a wife. He detached two girls from the group, seized them by the waist, and told them they must go with him as his wives. He then ordered the girls to cut him some tree bark for a fire. As the girls each struck a separate tree, the trees grew suddenly so that their tops reached the sky. The other five sisters, who were already in the sky, called out to the first two. At this point, the kidnapped pair quickly climbed up the trees, and were drawn into the heavens by their sisters to live with them forever.

(Just in passing, sir/madam—how could the Greek and Aborigine names for the hunter, Orion and Wurrunna, be anything other than, origin, *the same name,* the same word? How could this possibly be any kind of coincidence?)

Here now is the story of the Pleiades as told by the *American Indians of North America.* Seven young girls were being pursued by a bear. They tried to save themselves by climbing up onto a flat rock. But the bear could easily climb up this too. So the gods caused the rock to rise up and push the girls into the sky—where they still are as the seven stars of the Pleiades.

And finally, Geoffrey Ashe tells us (without giving all the details) that there is a *Jewish* legend concerning the origin of the Pleiades that also involves a bear pursuing seven girls, just as in the American Indian legend! So the Jews had the same basic story for the Pleiades as the American Indians! Well, well, well.

What more do we need to say?

The striking similarities among the three stories given are absolutely indisputable. There are always seven females, pursued by a hunter. These escape from their pursuer by divine and magical intervention.

They are placed out of reach forever in the sky, where they form the seven stars of the Pleiades.

These stories must absolutely, certainly, and indisputably come from one once-central (and authoritative) source. The marked differences in the details of the stories are, however, proof of a long, long separation from that once-central source.

But we are not done yet. Far from it.

Only three star constellations are named in the Bible (Old and New Testaments). These are—guess what?—Orion, the Pleiades, and the Great Bear. (Good heavens!) (Sorry!)

Various cultures and peoples all, obviously, name some or many of the star constellations. But again, the only three that are named by every major and minor culture *throughout the entire world and history* are Orion, the Pleiades, and the Great Bear. Just as in the Bible. And we should emphasize also that some primitive tribes name only these three.

But let's put even more emphasis on a further aspect of this situation. The Pleiades—just the Pleiades—are the *only* group worshipped—that's *worshipped—by every human group throughout all history*. Should we say that again? The *only* constellation worshipped by *every* human group throughout history.

Elaborate ceremonies are held in this connection. For example, the major religious ceremony of the Aztecs took place when the Pleiades was in the center of the sky at midnight, every fifty-two years. (Fifty-two just happens to be 4×13.) Then there was great rejoicing, because this meant that life on Earth could continue for another fifty-two years. The Pleiades also produces the most important ceremony of the year, every year, among other South American and North American peoples.

In Australia, the Aborigines, as with the Maoris, consider that the rising of the Pleiades above the horizon is the start of the New Year, and elaborate religious ceremonies are held. In Africa, the rising of the Pleiades is also celebrated as the New Year, as it is throughout the South Sea Islands. And so on, and so on, and so on.

The naturalist J. Walker Fawkes, writing in 1895, comments: "I cannot explain the Pleiades' significance or why of all stellar objects this minute cluster of stars of low magnitude is more important than any other stellar group."

One reason for its importance, I suggest, is that at the point when the Cro-Magnons entered (or rather invaded) Europe, the rising of Pleiades above the horizon signified the beginning of spring, and was probably worshipped at that time by Neanderthals for that reason. But that is scarcely an adequate explanation for the Pleiades' importance throughout the world—so a major puzzle remains here. (But, of course, and as ever, we are talking about a once-central and dominant source.)

Let's have a quick look at the constellation of the Great Bear.

Guess what? The Greeks, the Romans, the Babylonians, the Ainu of Japan, the Hindus, the American Indians, and many African tribes *all* call it the Great Bear. (Coincidence?)

We can certainly understand why Neanderthals would have called that constellation at the still center of the heavens (the North Pole), the Bear. (Though this is the *Little* Bear, not the *Great* Bear.) For it is the white polar bear that guards the North. White, of course, is the main color of the moon (and she controls the glaciers, the snow storms, ice caps, and so on). Don't forget that Neanderthals evolved through more than one ice age. And also, the fur of the white polar bear (and other bears) was certainly what protected Neanderthals from the cold—again, don't forget the bear-pelt factory in Hungary.

The bear, in fact, is indisputably another major moon animal. Mircea Eliade emphatically states that the bear is a lunar animal worldwide. He also goes on to say specifically that initiation ceremonies into manhood throughout the whole world involve the bear and the moon. That's ceremonies throughout the whole world . . . again! Once again. Yet again.

There is much more astronomical and astrological material we could present here in support of the central claims of this present book—for example, the striking similarities between the animals/creatures that are said to represent the four points of the compass in Egypt, Tibet, China, Mexico, and so on (see my book *Cities of Dreams*).

But instead, let's get to that actual first meeting of classic Neanderthals and Cro-Magnons.

Chapter 6

Cro-Magnon vs. Neanderthal—Then Cro-Magnon Plus Neanderthal

THE MEETING OF CLASSIC Neanderthals and Cro-Magnons in Europe some 35,000 years ago was an immense culture shock for both parties—though we are concerned mainly with its effects on the Cro-Magnons and their reaction to it. The two species were culturally opposite to each other in *every* way. (We'll say more about the role of opposites in nature when we come to the matter of genetics.)

Cro-Magnons were tall and athletic, creatures of the daylight and the open plains. They were hunters. In my further scenario, the male pair-bonded with one female for life. They worshiped the Sun. They were right-handed and far-sighted. They lived in colonies where each pair had their own small piece of territory.

Cro-Magnons evolved not in Africa—we'll get to the details of that particular rubbish from our academics toward the end of the book—but in Asia or India. And indeed, some of our otherwise hopeless anthropologists are now themselves beginning to come around to this view. In Asia, and unlike African apes, the gibbon ape pair-bonds with one female for life, lives in colonies where each pair has its own territory—around which the male parades aggressively each morning. The gibbon colony is, in fact, the perfect model for modern suburbia—"a man's home is his castle." Gibbons also sometimes band together to go hunting. And also, gibbons walk upright. They do not shamble along, as do chimpanzees and gorillas.

Neanderthals were short and barrel-bodied and had a shambling walk (as confirmed by many of the sightings of wild men; the Mongolian peasant report of 1970 states: "walks with knees bent, stoops, and is in-toed"). In my own further scenario, Neanderthals were nocturnal or seminocturnal. They were left-handed and nearsighted. Their society was led and dominated by the females, not, as in the case of the Cro-Magnons, by the males. Originally the Neanderthals were gatherers, although no doubt later they also ate animal flesh. (I suspect, however, that they did not hunt animals as did Cro-Magnons, but trapped them in various ways.) They were nomadic with no permanent dwelling sites.

Neanderthals must have been absolutely horrifying—and enraging—to Cro-Magnons. Lived by night. Ugly. Led by females. Not just totally sexually promiscuous (including, as I now think, pedophilic, as the bonobo chimpanzees demonstrate)—but their very religion was sex. Religious ceremonies were sexual orgies. Moreover, the moon that Neanderthal worshipped was in charge of the sun—the Cro-Magnon god. She executed him at the end of the year and then, purely out of her goodwill and power, graciously resurrected him.

The Neanderthals' general social conduct was also absolutely unacceptable. Thus we have in English the expressions "to welsh" and "to jew" (as already mentioned), whose use is now banned. These verbs mean to lie, to cheat, to steal, to not keep your word or honor your promises, to stab others in the back, to win at any cost and by any means available, and so on. (But these were perfectly acceptable and *normal* behaviors for Neanderthals! It's only the Cro-Magnon in us that condemns them—and says instead, my word is my bond, death before dishonor, practice what you preach, above board, up front, hold your head up high, stiff upper lip, and so forth.)

So Neanderthals, their culture, and their behavior were *totally* unacceptable to Cro-Magnons. "The bastards—they lower their heads in surrender, and then they charge at you!" The *detail* of the endless opposites in the two species is astonishing—as the last remark shows: when a Cro-Magnon lowered his head, it meant that he had surrendered; when a Neanderthal lowered his head, he was about to attack.

Yet while so much of Neanderthal culture and practice was totally abhorrent to the Cro-Magnons, there is no doubt at all that the Cro-Magnons were very impressed by other aspects of it—for example, as I have already suggested, the Neanderthals' extensive knowledge of herbs as cures for illness and disease. (I did not mention, as a further example of that, the fact that the willow tree is closely associated with witchcraft—and the willow just happens to be a natural source of aspirin.) There was also the use of the stone abacus to predict timings and movements of the star clusters. I think Cro-Magnons also now took on board for the first time the magical powers of the moon—and her direct role in such matters as pregnancy, fertility, and menstruation. Hence, among other matters, the importance of the number thirteen in subsequent cultures.

Like any invader and plunderer, Cro-Magnons had two concerns: (1) to destroy and get rid of the current occupiers and owners; (2) to take over and profit from their possessions and (in this case) knowledge. Specifically, the powers of the moon had to be taken away from women as such. But equally, the sun had to be protected from the moon.

This is why menstruating women and pubertal girls had to be so drastically secluded and punished. This was not simply to incapacitate them. They were *specifically* kept out of sunlight, and in darkness, *to protect the sun itself.*

There is, we must emphasize, no doubt whatsoever that Neanderthals and Cro-Magnons did come together and have close contact—something that was long denied by our anthropologists and academics. But recent finds (of tools and whatever) have forced everyone to agree that Neanderthals and Cro-Magnons *did* at one point occupy the same living space in Europe. There used to be even more vigorous denial that the two actually interbred—many "experts" claimed that their two sets of genes were too different to allow this. But finds both in Israel and in Portugal of the remains of individuals with absolutely clearly mixed physical characteristics of the two varieties have forced at least some academics and scientists to withdraw their opposition to interbreeding.

And guess what? The coming together (in particular the sexual coming together) of Neanderthal and Cro-Magnon is recorded in the Bible, as the following citations clearly show.

For example: "And there appeared to me two men exceeding tall, so that I never saw such on earth. Their faces were shining like the Sun" (Book of Enoch). And: "As grasshoppers we seemed to ourselves, and so we seemed to them" (Numbers).

In both these cases, that's Neanderthals talking, as far as I'm concerned.

Cro-Magnons quite certainly raped many Neanderthal women, and quite probably kept some of them as slaves and companions. (Perhaps we should mention, just in passing, that rape is a perfectly normal feature of life among the orangutans of Asia.) In the following excerpts, again as far as I'm concerned, "Sons of God" is a reference to Cro-Magnons, and "daughters of men" a reference to Neanderthals.

"The Sons of God took to wife such [of the daughters of men] as they chose" (Genesis). But much more crucial is the following: "When the Sons of God came into the daughters of men and they bore children to them . . . there . . . were the mighty men of old, the men of renown" (Genesis).

(This item, again as far as I'm concerned, is an absolutely clear reference to the "hybrid vigor" of the offspring produced by the crossing of the two varieties—a matter that we get to in detail in the next chapter.)

Calling Cro-Magnons "sons"—that is, male—and Neanderthals "daughters," female, is, of course, totally appropriate from my point of view. But I would say that we have here also a very *specific* statement. Very, very specific.

It is stating that the hybrids (that's you and me!) did not arise from Neanderthal men raping or having sex with Cro-Magnon women. For any Cro-Magnon female impregnated by a Neanderthal male would certainly have died giving birth, along with the offspring itself—*because of the large head of the baby*—a problem still very much with us today, of course. Neanderthals had much larger heads than Cro-Magnons, as we know. So we, the product of the crossing of Neanderthal and Cro-Magnon, are descended from Neanderthal *females* and Cro-Magnon *males*. (Is that yet another reason why, worldwide, the left is associated with the feminine?) So Genesis got it right! (Sorry!)

We end here with another very, very dramatic item referring to our dual ancestry, and again from Genesis. (*Genesis*, let's not fail to remember, means the Book of *Origins*.)

Rebekah has conceived twins, and they "struggle together within her." So she consults God about this problem, and God replies: "There are two *nations* within your womb, and the two people born of you shall be divided: the one shall be stronger than the other, the elder shall serve the younger." (Two *nations*!) Then Rebekah gives birth. And now, guess what? You will scarcely believe this. *The firstborn is covered all over with red hair.* Yes, covered all over with red hair. (A baby covered all over with red hair.)

What *can*, what could, this be except an absolutely clear reference to Neanderthal and Cro-Magnon? What else could it possibly be? We now know that Neanderthals were red-haired (and, in fact, like Zana and all the others, covered with red hair). So we have in Genesis a memory, once again, an actual memory, of our distant past and origins.

Later, the second born, Jacob, robs Esau (the one covered with red hair) of his birthright. And yes, the Cro-Magnons *did* rob the Neanderthals of their territory and culture. And that item *also* is further confirmed in detail in Jeremiah. The descendants of Esau (the first born, covered all over with red hair) are told by God: "Turn and flee and hide in any caves." And then God says: "Esau's children . . . will all perish and he will be no more."

Well done, God. You got the story right.

Chapter 7
You/We Are
a Hybrid Species

You can observe Neanderthal at any public gathering.

OSWALD SPENGLER

(AND DIMITRI BAYANOV, IGOR BOUTSEV,

LOREN EISELEY, AND MYSELF ALL AGREE!)

SOME OF US HAVE a big toe that is shorter than the second toe.

So what?

It just happens to be the case that every Neanderthal fossil foot so far found and every Neanderthal footprint so far found has the big toe shorter than the second toe. Every Cro-Magnon fossil foot and every Cro-Magnon footprint has the long big toe. Well, well.

It is also the case that some of us are left-handed, others of us are right-handed. Many men go bald or have a receding hairline. Others show no trace of baldness or receding hairline whatsoever. (And guess what? Yes, it is a proven statistical fact that left-handed men almost never go bald, while right-handed men very often do.) (So in this respect, at least, left-handedness is "feminine.") Some of us have the tall, broad-shouldered athletic build. Others have the short, barrel-bodied pyknic physique. And so on.

Do we have evidence that, for example, left-handed individuals are, on average, shorter than right-handed individuals? Effectively, we do. Left-handedness in Wales is double that found in England, and the Welsh are on average shorter than the English. You're not impressed with that? Well, you should be. Because the Chinese are also significantly shorter than Europeans—and the rate of left-handedness in China is again twice that of Europe. Enough for you?

Some further double items. Most people have in the palm of their hands the two separate so-called head and heart lines. But some of us (including myself, as it happens) have one deep line in the palm of the hand (instead of the other two) running straight across from side to side. This is the so-called simian line, the ape line, because all apes have it.

Some of us are nearsighted, some are farsighted. So is tallness associated with farsightedness, and short height associated with nearsightedness? It would seem to be the case. More Chinese are nearsighted than Europeans, and the former are, on average, shorter than the latter. Jews living in Europe, in *every* European country, have recently been shown to be more nearsighted than their European companions. And Jews are, on average, shorter than Europeans.

(Perhaps we should mention again that redheadedness is not uncommon among Jews—hence Danny "The Red" Cohn-Bendit, so-called not just because of his political views but his red hair. Remember also that the ancient Egyptians used to sacrifice redheaded individuals—so these were available. And most people will be surprised to learn that, as noted earlier, redheadedness is quite common among Australian Aborigines.)

Anyway, there are two points to emphasize here. First, would we expect to find such, let alone so *many,* differing characteristics in one single species? No, we would not (and of course *do* not, when we examine any species of animal). A still more important point is that, as we already *know,* some of the differing characteristics are found together in single individuals. The crucial question, though, is this. Do all the various opposing items tend to cluster together? In other words, if you have one item in what we'll call list A, will you also tend to have the others in that list? And the same also for the B list?

So we ask, do left-handed people show a greater incidence of the short big toe? We don't know. Do left-handed people show a greater incidence of the simian line in the palm of the hand? We don't know. (I'm not left-handed, by the way, but my brother was.)

My own claim, of course, is that we *are* talking about two *sets* of characteristics, and that any individual with one of the characteristics in question would also (tend to) show other characteristics from that same set.

Set 1, which we now list, is, of course—as I claim—the Neanderthal list. (And as it happens, we do already *know,* for example, that Neanderthals were short in height and had short big toes.) We have already discussed many of these items at various points in this book—others not so far mentioned will be discussed later.

Set 1: short height/short big toe/left-handedness/pyknic body type/prominent eyebrows/projecting brow ridges/ less male-pattern baldness in men/the simian line in the palm of the hand/nearsightedness/higher sex drive/greater fertility and more children/longer periods of sleep spent in dreaming /larger cerebellum (that's the back brain)/ better night vision/higher incidence of homosexuality, lesbianism, and pedophilia/higher incidence of degrees in the arts, lower incidence of degrees in the sciences/ higher incidence of redheadedness/greater susceptibility to hypnosis.

(So, lots of research projects for you there, students!)

We'll stop there for the moment.

Now I'm going to mention just in passing here a very significant point concerning the matters under discussion. My proposals in this area arouse a great deal of fanatical opposition (as does my work in general, of course). The idea that these characteristics in society we individually and personally hate and condemn are in fact as important and justifiable and defensible as those characteristics we personally support is greatly upsetting for the majority of people. As is the idea that we are *each* two different people in one body ("two souls in one breast," as Faust put it).

So, for example, a leading consultant at the Royal Free Hospital in London agreed to look at the patients to see if left-handedness and the short big toe went together. He was ordered to stop by the hospital authorities. Gail Vines, who was the biology editor of the *New Scientist,* agreed to carry out a survey of the journal's readership. The project was vetoed by the editorial board. Another journalist resigned from his job with a leading magazine (I have to withhold the details here) when they refused to publish an interview he did with me about my views. (Part of this interview is included in appendix 1.) A student of the Catholic College for Further Education, where she gave a lecture, who was herself left-handed, volunteered to do a survey of her fellow students—she was sure, for instance, that there was a big incidence of left-handed men—was ordered to stop the survey or be expelled. Boris Johnson, the editor of the *Spectator,* commissioned an article from me concerning our political scenario (which we get to shortly). He himself was delighted with the article—but his advisors and colleagues told him not to publish—and so he didn't.

(So what does this tell us about the board of the Royal Free Hospital, the Catholic College of Further Education, the *New Scientist,* the *Spectator?* It says we should get rid of all of them!)

We shall shortly be looking at specifically biological matters—but before that, let's examine one more major "double."

Throughout the whole world we have two opposed political parties—the left wing (communists, Labour, Democrat) and the right wing (Fascist, Conservative, Republican, and so on.) These have diametrically opposed views.

Thus Labour (in Britain) is pro-gay, pro-single mothers, anti-marriage, soft on crime, soft on education, pro-feminist, pro-working class, and so forth. Conservatives are pro-marriage, anti-gay, tough on crime, strict on education, anti-feminist, anti-single mothers, pro-elitism, pro-aristocracy/monarchy, and the like. All these attributes and attitudes are well known and accepted—though I have expressed them rather bluntly and crudely here. And, of course, *in fact,* there are more women who are members of the Labour Party than are members of the Conservative Party, more Labour Parliamentary Members and electoral candidates who are women than is the case with the Conservatives, and so on.

Anyway, my own question, of course, is: Are there more left-handed people among members of the Labour Party than among member of the Conservative Party? I say the answer is yes—though hard statistics are not available. For, as we know, the rate of left-handedness in Wales is double that found in England. And guess what? All Welsh Members of the British Parliament are Labour. There is not one Conservative Welsh MP. And the local Welsh Assembly in Wales is itself Labour dominated.

Also, the rate of left-handedness in China, as again we know, is double that found in Europe. And China just happens to be a communist state! Well, well, well.

I think also that most people, if asked, would consider, like myself, that more individuals in the arts (such as actors) would vote Labour than Conservative. And guess what—the rate of left-handedness among arts graduates just happens to be 15 percent, whereas the rate of left-handedness among science graduates is only 4 percent.

So the *inference* of my claim is clear. But, of course, we do need hard statistics about the voting tendencies of left-handers.

And my further claim, obviously, is that *all* the items of Set 1 above (the Neanderthal list) would be more frequently found among members of the Labour Party than among members of the Conservative Party. (I stress here that I am specifying members of these two parties—and so excluding the independent "swing" voter.)

Short height, for instance? Well, I'm quite sure that the members of the working class in Britain are, on average, shorter than the upper classes and the aristocracy. And the *voting* tendencies of these groups overall are, of course, quite clear.

But let's get back to the main, amazing fact that we have, world-wide, two diametrically opposed political parties.

Why on earth should this be the case?

If, say, lions evolved to a high level of consciousness and intelligence, surely they would have only one party—the Lion Party. *All* lions would agree with/to the basic rules of their society. If horses evolved, surely we would simply have the Horse Party; if elephants, the Elephant Party. Wouldn't we? *Wouldn't* we? Why should there be, why would there be, two sets of diametrically opposed views among evolved elephants?

Time now to say that both orthodox biology and the practice of animal breeding both offer dramatic support for my general position.

It is totally proven and accepted that when *widely separated* varieties of animals are crossed (in the laboratory or in the farmyard), their offspring possess *opposing pairs* of instinctive urges, between which the animal has great difficulty in choosing.

And they also possess *new* behaviors and qualities possessed by *neither* of the parents.

The peach-faced lovebird, when in the process of building a nest, tears off strips of bark and leaves for this purpose. These it tucks into its rump feathers before flying to the nest site.

The Fischer's lovebird, however, when nest-building, holds this same material in its beak when flying back to the nest site.

But the hybrid cross between these two varieties of lovebird is found to possess the instinctive qualities of *both* its parents. So this (unfortunate!) offspring, when preparing to build a nest, tears off a strip of bark or a leaf. Its peach-faced instinct tells it to stuff the strip into its rump feathers, which it does. Then it gets ready to fly. But at this point its Fischer instinct says, "Hang on, you're supposed to have the nest material in your beak." So the bird now pulls the item from its rump feathers, holds it in its beak, and gets ready to fly. But now its peach-faced ancestry intervenes: "Hey, you shouldn't have that in your beak, it's supposed to be in your rump feathers." So now once again the bird tucks the material into its back feathers. But yet again the Fischer instinct objects. "No, in your mouth, stupid." And once again the bird pulls the material out of its back plumage.

The process goes on and on and on. The bird, now exhibiting clear signs of confusion and helplessness, is permanently stuck in this state of nonresolution.

Does that remind you of anyone? Does it? (No, I'm not joking.)

There are plenty of examples of these double, conflicting behaviors, these no-clear-choice situations among hybrid animals.

Hybrids that exhibit these conflicting behaviors are, in fact, dumped by the animal breeders. That's a great pity. If we allowed these confused hybrids to go on breeding, we might get some useful information about our own position. Because it is *absolutely clear* that *we*—the hybrid cross between Cro-Magnon and Neanderthal—have exactly such pairs of opposing instincts.

And that is why (apart from all the other evidence) we have so many metaphors on this subject: two souls within one breast/the divided self/ the head wanting one thing, the heart wanting another/having your cake and eating it/six of one and half a dozen of another/a bet each way/between a rock and a hard place/running with the hare and hunting with the hounds/two-faced/turning a blind eye/double-dealing/in two minds/two-timing/saying one thing and doing another/having it both ways—and so on and so on.

This is why, to take one more example, so many of us long for one everlasting love (and we *do* mean it) on the one hand, but can't resist a bit on the side when the opportunity presents itself. (That's pair-bonding versus promiscuity, of course.) And this particular situation was fully recognized in French society in recent times. A married man was publicly allowed to have a mistress, or to visit a prostitute, providing he made the matter fully known to his wife. (Well, well.)

That French approach was/is actually our best solution—to acknowledge and accept our basic duality and so avoid the consequences of denying our duality—a denial that solves nothing, because we go on "cheating" anyway, at least from time to time, and notably in times of great pressure and interactions of great temptation.

Now we turn to the second phenomenon—the fact that when two widely separated species crossbreed, the offspring frequently possess new abilities, behaviors, and qualities *possessed by neither of the parents*. Did you hear that? *Possessed by neither of the parents*.

And that is precisely what professional animal and plant breeding is all about.

Biologists have recently agreed, incidentally, that when such crossing occurs in nature due to some unusual set of circumstances, then a *new species* is produced overnight.

So, Darwin, I'm afraid you got that bit wrong. Nature *does* proceed by leaps. Or to use your terminology: *natura* does *facit saltum*. Now, guess what else? Neither Neanderthal nor Cro-Magnon culture had shown *any* advance or change for tens upon tens of thousands of years. No advance or change. Both species were static and unchanging.

But then, some 35,000 years ago, at the point when Cro-Magnons entered Europe, we have a sudden explosion in the range and complexity of tools. That is a *fact*. And in no time at all—in the blink of an eye, in evolutionary terms—our modern civilization starts to emerge.

The genetic crossing of Cro-Magnon and Neanderthal produced not just (a) highly gifted individuals ("the mighty men of old, the men of renown") but (b) *an entirely new species of human*—ourselves.

Natura had made a huge *saltum*.

As I have already said, this new product was, in my view, either entirely or very largely due to Cro-Magnon men fertilizing Neanderthal women—not the other way around.

These offspring would have been accepted into Cro-Magnon groups. They were, after all, the sons and daughters of Cro-Magnon males. (Though it is also possible that some of the hybrids set up their own groups.)

And so Neanderthal genes were introduced into the Cro-Magnon gene pool—not in massive amounts initially. When one of the *hybrids* mated with a pure Cro-Magnon, obviously their offspring would have been only one-quarter Neanderthal. Nevertheless, those with Neanderthal genes (and, of course, with the new kind of genes) would have been not just more sexually active but more *fertile* than pure Cro-Magnons.

So as time went by, the Neanderthal genes in the general pool would have increased. And so would the Neanderthal "influence"—the *behavioral* influence—have greatly increased.

And that is why, during historical times, in all countries, we have seen the gradual rise and increase of left-wing groups as opposed to right-wing groups. Culminating, of course, in the actual French Revolution and the Russian Revolution—where the aristocracy, and the monarchs, were overthrown by "the people."

My claims here, as I've repeatedly said, could be readily confirmed—or not!—by surveys showing that left-wing individuals have more characteristics from the Neanderthal than they have Cro-Magnon characteristics, and vice-versa for right-wing individuals. And, by the way, we have by no means finished with the items on these respective lists.

(May I also just state here that I would be very interested to see the results of a comparative examination of the characteristics of the Brahmin caste in India with the characteristics of the Untouchable caste? These for me, again, represent, respectively, our Cro-Magnon and Neanderthal duality.)

We come now to part 2 of this book, which is specifically concerned with brain function. But this scenario fully ties in with the scenario we have already established.

PART TWO

Our Missing Psychology

Chapter 8

Cerebrum and Cerebellum

WE HAVE ALREADY MENTIONED the brain organ known as the cerebellum. This is our rear brain buried at the back of the head. The forebrain is called the cerebrum. "Cerebellum" actually means little cerebrum.

The cerebellum is, indeed, smaller than the cerebrum—but is by no means as small as it might at first appear. By reason of its deeply folded, walnut-like structure, and in terms of its surface area (that's cortex), the cerebellum is actually *three-quarters the size* of the cerebrum. To repeat this, the cerebellum has three-quarters as much cortex as the cerebrum. And the cortex of the *cerebrum* is where all our daytime conscious mental activity takes place.

As we proceed now, two items to keep very much in mind are: (1) that Neanderthals had a much larger cerebellum than Cro-Magnons, and (2) that women have a much larger cerebellum than men.

Now we move to a truly amazing item. This matter is a *fact*, an undisputed fact. Yet, when, students, did you ever hear or read about this matter (still less get any kind of explanation)? Answer: Never.

The fact is that a direct ancestor of ours (and all mammals), a lizard-like creature, had two pairs of eyes. Yes, *two pairs of eyes*. One pair was placed on top of the head and connected to the cerebellum. The second pair was in front and connected to the cerebrum.

Originally the cerebellum, with its eyes on top of the head, was the dominant brain. But in the course of further time—and why, we do not know—the main front brain, the cerebrum, and its pair of eyes gradually took over command.

The pair of eyes on the top of the head now fused together and sank down into the skull to form the pineal gland. The pineal gland is still light sensitive in ourselves today. (And you will never guess what—the ancient Hindus, 3,000 years ago, named the pineal gland "the third eye," the eye of mysticism and clairvoyance. How did the ancient Hindus, who, of course, had no knowledge whatsoever of our evolutionary past, reach this amazing conclusion?)

We go on here to list many of the absolutely remarkable facts concerning the cerebellum. But first, I want to stress the total exclusion of the cerebellum (and many associated matters) from our psychology textbooks in particular—but equally from our biological/scientific/educational scenario in general. Just (as we have seen) as is also the case with Neanderthals and their culture and their impact on our present lives.

In 1984, I did a survey of the leading psychology textbooks used on university degree courses. Lindzey, Hall, and Thompson's *Psychology* had 2 pages on the cerebellum out of a total of 762 pages. Smith, Sarason, and Sarason's *Psychology: The Frontiers of Behaviour* had 2 pages on the cerebellum out of a total of 658 pages. Hilgard and Atkinson's *Introduction to Psychology* had 2 out of 587 pages. McConnell's *Understanding of Behaviour* had 1 out of 780 pages (!). In case you are wondering, physiological-psychology textbooks were no better. Carlson's *The Psychology of Behaviour* had 4 out of 690 pages. Thompson's *Foundations of Physiological Psychology* had 7 out of 625 pages. Grossman's *Textbook of Physiological Psychology* had 15 out of 890 pages. (Well done, Grossman!)

During the 60 million years or so during which the cerebrum has developed and come to prominence, the cerebellum has *also* continued to evolve, and dramatically so. Like the cerebrum, it has produced its own two hemispheres. And whereas in more primitive creatures, the cerebrum and the cerebellum share their sensory pathways (to various parts of the body, the midbrain, and lower parts of the brain), *in mammals*—and, of course, *in ourselves*—the cerebellum has evolved its own sensory pathways. It is, in this sense, completely independent of the cerebrum. Even more significantly, women have a greater number of these new and independent pathways than men. So the cerebellum in women is significantly more evolved than in men.

(And so, guess what? A female rat with the cerebrum entirely removed can nevertheless mate, produce offspring, and rear them. A male with the cerebrum removed cannot even have sex. So the cerebellar differences between female and male in mammals are clearly very important.)

From several points of view, the cerebellum is actually more highly developed than the cerebrum (in both sexes). For example, the Purkinje cells of the cerebellum can individually form as many as 100,000 interconnections—far more than any other cells in the nervous system. A typical figure for cells in the cerebrum is 1,000 interconnections. There are also more cells in the granular layer of the cerebellar cortex than in the *whole* of the rest of the brain!

A further point is that the cerebellum receives massive input from all areas of the cerebrum, in particular from the cerebral cortex, which is considered to be the seat of waking consciousness.

When a sensory receptor (such as the eye or the ear) is stimulated, this stimulation produces organized patterns of projections in the cerebral cortex. This response is believed to be associated with consciousness. But *precisely* these patterns are also produced in the cerebellar cortex. So are they associated with some form of consciousness in the cerebellum? The question is never asked or answered.

Before moving on to further matters concerning the cerebellum, we should first clear away any remnants of the "split brain" theory that may still be in the reader's mind.

The split-brain theory of Roger Sperry, Robert Ornstein, and Michael Gazzaniga dominated psychological thinking during the second half of the last century—and for it, Roger Sperry was actually awarded the Nobel Prize.

I myself said at the time that the theory was fundamentally flawed (in my book *The Double Helix of the Mind* and in a number of articles, including one in the *New Scientist*). The two halves of the cerebrum, on which the theory was based, do *not* in *any* sense form the duality of conscious–unconscious, or any other duality. The two halves of the cerebrum, in fact, have *no secrets from each other whatsoever*. Yes, different faculties—such as language—are located in one or the other hemisphere. But this is purely and absolutely a matter of making best use of the available "office space."

For, as is now fully agreed, both halves of the cerebrum have *total access to all each other's information* and can each perform any task or function whatsoever. Thus a person who has one or the other hemisphere surgically removed for medical reasons retains *all* his or her mental and physical faculties (although, yes, adults may experience a temporary loss of faculties—you have to relocate the furniture in the now-available office space!). And very, very significantly, there is no change of handedness. No matter which hemisphere is removed, a right-handed person remains right-handed, a left-handed person remains left-handed.

We need not go on here, because the split-brain theory of Sperry and the others was officially dumped by the scientific establishment in 2000. I, of course, had already said it *should* be dumped more than twenty years earlier. The *New Scientist* did briefly acknowledge that I had got there first—but as was the case with my discovery/claim of Neanderthal redheadedness, which we dealt with in part 1, I once again received no general acknowledgement of my preemptive work from the scientific and academic establishments.

So we are now free to concentrate on the *real division*, the *real* duality of human psychology, namely the cerebrum versus the cerebellum—and the many, many matters associated therewith.

Chapter 9

Some of the Creative Powers of the Cerebellum

THE MATTERS THAT FOLLOW are, like those of the previous chapter, totally excluded by our psychological establishment. But, of course, these should be absolutely *central* matters of consideration. In fact, they compose 50 percent of our being. So current academic psychology *excludes* 50 percent of our being, 50 percent of our *real life*.

Let me make it clear at this point that I am totally qualified—never mind totally justified—to criticize psychologists and mainstream psychology and make this protest.

After obtaining a degree in psychology, I was appointed senior research psychologist at the National Children's Bureau (my first job as a psychologist!). During my time there, apart from conducting various investigations and publishing numerous papers, I coauthored two textbooks on child development, both of which became required reading in university courses.

When I stated my intention to leave the National Children's Bureau to pursue my career as a writer, I was offered the post of Director of the National Bureau and also that of Professor of Psychology at Brunel University. (But my heart was set on writing full-time.)

So in no way can I be accused of being any kind of outsider, or of being uninformed on the matters in question, by members of the psychological establishment. (Incidentally, I also had two full years of psychoanalysis—Jungian—a qualification that the very large majority of psychologists do not have.)

We turn now to a list of items, all of which interconnect and interact. And a point to very much stress is that in all cases, women figure more prominently than men, often dramatically so.

DREAMING

As already indicated, women dream more than men. (They also sleep more, but nevertheless, a greater proportion of that sleeping time is spent in dreaming than is the case with men.)

Where shall we begin?

During 90 percent of dreaming time, men have an erection of the penis, and women an erection of the clitoris. Did you know that, sir/ madam? We have here a full arousal of the sex organs during 90 percent of dreaming. But, of course, scarcely any of the dream content, of the events of the dream, have anything to do with sex.

Arousal of the sex organs is a function of the autonomic nervous system—that is, of the cerebellum. We cannot produce an erection by conscious will or instruction. All we can do in this respect is to start thinking of sexual images—and then the cerebellum obliges by producing an erection.

Moving on, electrical stimulation of the cerebellum produces the twitches of the face and limbs we observe when an individual is dreaming. And animals with the *cerebrum* totally removed nevertheless continue to display the usual cycle of dreaming. That is, they continue to dream.

The foregoing items are effectively conclusive proof of the involvement of the cerebellum in dreaming. You haven't forgotten, have you, that women have a larger cerebellum than men? But we have plenty more evidence on this account.

Dreaming begins with mammals. Shall we repeat *that*? Dreaming begins with mammals. Animals below mammals on the evolutionary scale—such as reptiles—*do not dream*. And it is, of course, precisely with mammals, as already discussed, that the cerebellum and the cerebrum evolve into two separate organs, each with its own nervous system. And with this new independence of the cerebellum, dreaming begins. (Just a coincidence?)

It is clear, expressing this matter in metaphorical terms, that the cerebellum and the cerebrum made a deal. The cerebellum said to the cerebrum, "Okay, you get daylight consciousness and waking activity. But I'll be conscious and active during the night, while you take time off." "Fair enough," said the cerebrum. "Oh, one more thing," said the cerebellum. "I also get *full* access to *all your* conscious information and memories." "Oh, very well," said the cerebrum.

This last point is no fantasy. As I said earlier, the cerebellum receives *massive input* from all areas of the cerebral cortex. But there is still more.

During nondreaming sleep, the muscles of the body are fully relaxed, and the cerebrum itself is dormant. But during dreaming, the muscles become effectively paralyzed—and it is far harder to rouse an individual from dreaming sleep than from nondreaming sleep. And yet—and yet—guess what?—the cerebral cortex is *now* reactivated. And most impressively still, we now also get rapid eye movement. *Our eyes are watching the dream.* Our eyes are watching the dream. But the information and abilities of the cerebral cortex are not being used in their *normal way*—not logically or sensibly. They are being used in weird combinations, illogically, associatively, magically, emotionally, and so forth. They are being used as "the stuff of dreams"—and we all know how "mad" and "pointless" dreams can be.

Experiments have been conducted in which sleeping individuals are aroused from sleep as soon as they begin dreaming (shown by rapid eye movements and other indicators.). They are then allowed to go to sleep again.

After two or three nights of this treatment, the individuals concerned become really disturbed. They are getting enough sleep, but they are being deprived of dreaming. To use metaphorical terms again—the cerebellum is shouting: "Hey! I'm not having this! Our agreement is that I had consciousness and control at night—you can't take that away from me. That's our bloody agreement!"

Leaving aside the metaphorical, what is totally clear from these experiments is that dreaming is *absolutely essential* to normal mental health. Deprived of dreaming, we become seriously mentally disturbed.

Dreams also have other very strong credentials.

Many writers, artists, composers, and other creative individuals have stated categorically that some (or all) of their inspiration arises *directly* in dreams. Robert Louis Stevenson, for example, dreamed the story of *Dr. Jekyll and Mr. Hyde,* and Coleridge dreamed *Kublai Khan.* Others who have publicly announced major dream sourcing include de Quincy, Lindsay Kemp, Joan Grant, Peter Redgrove, Penelope Shuttle, and many others. (I have only one instance of this phenomenon in my own experience—I dreamed a science fiction story, "A Time for Living," that was published in a Corgi paperback collection, now out of print.)

So even on the basis of what we have seen so far, no half-brained scientist can say that dreams are unimportant, meaningless rubbish. As, nevertheless, the very large majority of them *do* say!

A further remarkable item is lucid dreaming. In the state of lucid dreaming, the events of the dream proceed as usual—they are as strange, weird, and wonderful as they always are. But you are there as your normal self-conscious self! You are visiting the dream world as your fully conscious self. You are a tourist, so to speak. You are who you normally are, and you *know* that you are dreaming. It is an amazing experience. But it is also clear evidence that dreaming is *a fully independent* self-governing process. It is quite separate from and fully independent of our normal conscious mind and *its* processes. Dreaming is a "reality" on its own terms and in its own territory—an alternative reality.

Lucid dreaming can be induced by various exercises. My own lucid dreaming, however, began spontaneously during my twenties, in a context we will be examining in the next chapter.

One more item in this section.

In 1971, the *American Journal of Psychiatry* published a study of a random sample of adult males concerning the time spent in dreaming and sleeping. The study found that the males fell into two distinct groups—we should underline, *two:* one group spent significantly longer in sleep and in dreaming time, and also dreamed more intensively (as shown by brain activity) than the other.

The members of the group that slept and dreamed significantly *less,* and also dreamed less intensively, were conformist and establishment oriented, both in the opinions they expressed and in the nature of their work. The members of the other group (the dreamers) were in general nonconformist, and they included not just a number of creative artists, but several drop-out hippies.

These findings are, of course, an absolutely significant vindication—they are proof—that left-wingers (Neanderthals) dream more than right-wingers (Cro-Magnons). For can we doubt for a moment what the actual political voting choices of these two groups would have been?

TRANCE, HYPNOSIS, SLEEPWALKING, AND AUTOMATIC WRITING

There are other alternative states, all interrelated and not unrelated to dreaming. And also, once again, to the cerebellum. (There is also the matter of mediumistic trance, but that particular item will be considered in the next chapter.)

Sleepwalking we will deal with just briefly. This is not simply a matter of stumbling around the bedroom while still asleep and unconscious. Sleepwalkers have been observed (by reliable witnesses) to get up and, for example, prepare and cook themselves a meal, eat it, and then go back to bed. The most dramatic case of all involved a man who got into his car, drove to the supermarket, did the shopping, and returned home.

In regard to the matters we can now come to, it must be stressed— cannot be overstressed—that the events involve many totally reliable witnesses, such as doctors, psychologists, and psychoanalysts, often more than one such witness in a particular case. Of the many hundreds of cases on proven and reliable record (apart from the tens of thousands reported informally), several have been published in medical and psychological journals.

We are not talking of any kind of speculation here, any kind of fraud or lying or fantasy. We are talking *facts*. Let's say that again. Facts.

My own main concern here is to indicate the role of the cerebellum in these matters.

We'll begin with automatic writing. What happens here is that a person who has been hypnotized, or has gone into self-induced trance, begins writing messages and texts. These are involuntary, not in any way deliberate or consciously controlled. (Many psychic mediums also do this in their trance states—but, as said, we get specifically to mediums in the next chapter.)

So how do we know that the person involved is not faking what he or she is doing? Well, for instance, some individuals write *backward* and sometimes at great speed, with all the letters and words reversed. This is mirror-writing—hold a normally written or printed sentence up to a mirror, and you will see the product in question. Also, try writing backward consciously yourself. It will be a very, very slow process, and you will make many, many mistakes. The automatic writer makes no mistakes.

Some people write two different texts using both hands simultaneously! Sometimes a person, while producing automatic writing, will read aloud from a book! Or the writer's hands may be completely hidden from his or her view by a newspaper or cloth. That the writing concerned *is* automatic, is self-governing, cannot, therefore, in any way be disputed. But there is still more.

Dr. Anita Mühl, a hospital psychiatrist, has studied and published much case material of this kind in connection with her patients and the following examples are taken from her work. In one of her experiments, Mühl read aloud several paragraphs from a story that the patient had never heard before. Then, while herself reading aloud from a newspaper, the patient concerned now wrote out the paragraphs she had just heard once, spelling all the words *backward,* without any mistakes or omissions!!

This is all absolutely amazing. But of still greater interest, from my own point of view, is that Mühl's patients, along with many other automatic writers, sometimes produce stories and poems. *Good* stories and poems. So we have a clear link here with artistic creativity.

This last item and connection is further underlined by the example of Mrs. John Curran, an everyday housewife. She began practicing automatic writing, just out of interest. Then she began writing "automatic novels." She subsequently published several (historical) novels under the name of Patience Worth—the spirit who she believed was writing through her.

There is more than just the phenomenon of automatic writing—we also have automatic drawing, automatic painting, automatic composing, automatic singing, and so on.

Luis Gasperetto, working in trance at great speed, produces drawings and paintings in the quite unmistakable styles of Picasso, Rembrandt, Modigliani, and others. Sometimes he works using both hands at once. Sometimes he produces paintings upside down.

Matthew Manning demonstrates a similar ability—but even more remarkable. Art experts *cannot* distinguish between Manning's work, produced in trance, and that of the real artist concerned.

Rosemary Brown—once again, an everyday housewife—writes

music in trance unmistakably and impressively in the style of Beethoven, Mozart, Strauss, Liszt, and so on. She herself believes that the music is dictated to her by the spirits of the dead composers. But in any case, her work is widely acclaimed by the critics. There exist two CDs of her music, and it is increasingly performed at concerts. There are also two volumes of this music in manuscript form.

A man calling himself Caruso, because he believes himself to be a reincarnation of the singer Enrico Caruso, in trance sings so much like the real Caruso that he makes his living from it, performing publicly.

Let us mention in passing here that real, professional musicians and singers themselves play better and sing better under hypnosis than they do in their normal waking state and professional lives.

Turning once again to Dr. Mühl's patients, a young woman was hospitalized after being rescued from an attempted suicide by drowning. The woman had a lifelong history of mental illness (coupled with physical illness) that culminated in the severe mental fragmentation known as multiple personality.

This patient could produce automatic writing, automatic speaking, and automatic piano playing. Although when playing the piano in the normal waking state she was only a mediocre player, when in trance she played beautifully.

In one of her sessions with Dr. Mühl, the woman's left hand was playing the piano. At the same time her right hand wrote: "The heart of a lily may be pure but its feet are sometimes sucked by the mire."

At the same time again she spoke these words: "Eyes, eyes, I see a cerebellum, anatomically speaking, physiologically and psychologically a brain—maybe it's food for worms. Maybe it's cultural—planted like seed—food for humanity. We're put here to propagate—just to feed worms. Some think I am this, you are this. We are this. We are just tiny bits of atoms with a cerebellum."

I consider that the patient was informing us here that the origin of the unconscious and creative mind (and specifically her own quite distinct personalities) is the cerebellum. (Perhaps she was a fan of mine!)

There is, further, the matter of changes in facial expression by individuals working or composing or performing in trance, or under hypnosis. These connect with many reports that when, say, a middle-aged person in trance is recalling incidents of their childhood—or when "possessed" by the "spirit" of a young person (as with mediums in trance)—the face smoothes out and wrinkles disappear, and we have the face of a youngster. Conversely, a young person in trance, when retelling details of an alleged "past life" as an elderly person, now develops the haggard, wrinkled face of an old person. We should also stress here the *suddenness* with which these changes occur.

Only our autonomic system, of course—that is, the cerebellum—could/can produce such changes. We cannot consciously cause such things to happen. So once again, here is *proof* of the involvement of the cerebellum.

And just one more solid piece of proof here that we are dealing with the cerebellum and the autonomic nervous system. A woman with appendicitis was hypnotized and asked about her condition. She said that she had a piece of bone lodged in her appendix. The doctor then asked her if she could remove it. She now squeezed the bone out of her appendix and into the colon and then moved it on through the colon—meanwhile speaking of what she was doing and describing where the bone was in her colon. Then finally she ejected the bone out through her anus. A real piece of bone.

If the reports so far seem unlikely, they pale into insignificance beside the following items—items confirmed *again* and *again* by doctors, psychiatrists, and psychologists—and sometimes reported in professional journals. This first example, for instance, was reported, with photographs, in the *Lancet*.

A patient suffered from persistent sleepwalking. Hospitalized for this condition, he had had his arms tied behind his back in an attempt to prevent the condition occurring. But nevertheless he sleepwalked again and tore his arms free. His wrists were now badly wealed and bleeding.

Ten years later, while having psychotherapy, he was given the drug

Evipan. He became dissociated and began reciting poetry. Then he placed his arms behind his back and began struggling and gasping. Under the gaze of the watching doctor, the welts and the bleedings of ten years earlier now *spontaneously reappeared!*

A woman had as a girl been savagely beaten by her sadistic father. She had a mental breakdown at the age of seventeen and suffered from severe amnesia. Her emotional problems continued throughout her life, and at the age of thirty-seven she came into the care of a London psychiatrist. During her psychotherapy sessions, she would often go into a trance state. In these trances she gave much detail of the beatings her father had given her.

But as she described the specific wounds the whippings had produced, the bleeding wounds now appeared on her legs, buttocks, shoulders, hands—under the gaze of her psychiatrist. These were photographed as they appeared. On one occasion another doctor was present, and he confirmed that the wounds appeared spontaneously and instantly. These wounds were manifested *on thirty different occasions.* They were wholly real and had to be dressed and treated like any normal wounds.

Dr. Raymond Moody reports a case where a patient talked of being thrashed with a whip as a child by her father. Large bruises, which then began bleeding, appeared on her buttocks and shoulders. These had to be immediately treated. But Dr. Moody also writes that the wounds healed remarkably rapidly.

The housekeeper (Elizabeth) of the psychiatrist Alfred Lechler was a former patient who (as in one of our earlier examples) had suffered from multiple personality. One day Elizabeth returned home from a Good Friday lecture concerned with the crucifixion of Christ. She complained of severe pains in her hands and feet. Lechler now hypnotized Elizabeth, but instead of telling her the pains would go away, he said that they would get worse, and that nails were being forced into her extremities. (Lucky he wasn't *your* psychiatrist!) Now she produced red, swollen, bleeding marks on her palms and feet.

Lechler explained to the now-awake Elizabeth that he had given her the instructions in order to help her understand her condition. He asked her if she could weep tears of blood. A few hours later, blood began welling from her eyes. In a later experiment, he told her she was wearing a crown of thorns. Next morning, Elizabeth had bleeding puncture marks in her forehead.

All the phenomena mentioned were photographed by Lechler.

There are *many, many* other cases of deeply religious individuals reproducing the wounds of Christ, in full view of onlookers including doctors, on their hands, feet, and other parts of their bodies, whenever they turn their minds to these issues. On full record, for example, is the case of a religious girl who began bleeding spontaneously from her left palm during Easter week. Taken to a doctor, she began to produce bleeding wounds on her feet, chest, and forehead, under his observation.

A very important point to make here is that these individuals produce bleeding wounds *in the palms of their hands.* Today we *know* that, in fact, Christ was nailed to the cross through the *wrists,* and not through the palms of his hands. So in no way were/are these individuals possessed by the spirit of Christ or some angel—as they believed and claimed, and as they believe and claim today. Their own minds were producing the wounds, using the false information about crucifixion that they had been given. (The "brides of Christ," incidentally, often produce a red ring on the stem of their wedding finger!)

In fully authenticated *experiments,* hypnotized individuals have been told that they were being touched with stinging nettles—but they were, in fact, being touched or rubbed with ordinary plant leaves. The subjects then produced on their bodies the blisters that nettles normally produce. Others were rubbed with real nettle leaves but were told they were harmless chestnut leaves. They produced no blisters at all! In another experiment, a man was told he was being touched with a red-hot poker (it was actually perfectly cold). He produced a large blister filled with blood. A woman, who was not touched with *anything* at all, produced such blisters on various parts of her body after merely being *told* she had been touched with a red-hot poker.

Many of the foregoing items could be classified as "self-harming." Here now an instance of self-healing. Confronted with just this one piece of evidence, any half-brained scientist, any half-brained academic, any half-brained sceptic who persists in denying the validity of the matters we are discussing should be publicly prosecuted in court, dismissed from his or her post, and sent to prison. (No, I'm serious!)

Dr. Alexis Carrell was a distinguished scientist and Nobel Prize winner in medicine who died in 1944. In 1902, Carrell became interested in the question of psychic healing, and in 1903 he took charge of a group of patients visiting the shrine of Lourdes. In the group was one of Carrell's own patients, Marie Bailly—all this girl's family had already died of tuberculosis, and she was in the last stages of tubercular peritonitis. The girl's condition and prognosis of imminent death—she had *hours* rather than *days* left to live—had been confirmed independently by two other doctors. She had tuberculosis lesions in her lungs, disseminated tuberculosis throughout her system, and tubercular sores on her body. In this condition, she now arrived at Lourdes.

At this point the numerous watchers saw a truly miraculous change. Marie's pulse and respiration returned to normal. Her distended abdomen shrank. Her coloring normalized.

Carrell and *three other* doctors then examined and clinically tested Marie that same evening. Not the *slightest* doubt or reservation was expressed by any of them. Marie was totally and permanently free from every trace of disease.

Carrell publicly declared his belief in "miraculous healing." *For this he was sacked from his post at the Lyons Faculty of Medicine.* He then left France and took up a post at the Rockefeller Institute in New York. For his work *there* he received the Nobel Prize for medicine in 1912.

This is an appropriate moment to move to the matter of psychic healing.

There are many reported cases, confirmed by reliable witnesses, of the ability of some individuals to heal wounds and cure illnesses in other people far more rapidly than can any medication by the "laying on of hands."

Fortunately, we have absolute *proof* of this situation via a number of controlled experiments in laboratories using animals.

In one large-scale laboratory experiment conducted by Dr. Bernard Grad at Canada's McGill University, a psychic healer, Oskar Estebany, produced significantly faster healing in experimentally wounded mice, not by actually touching them, but simply by placing his hands against their cages for a few minutes each day. Control groups of mice were (a) treated by medical staff in the same way or (b) not treated at all. Both showed a much lower rate of improvement than those treated by Estebany.

In later experiments, Estebany caused plants to grow faster, taller, and with more leaves (than the control plants) simply by healing the solution with which the plants were fed. Later again (at the Human Dimensions Institute in New York), he raised pancreatic enzyme, denatured by exposure to a magnetic field, back to its useful level of functioning.

Another (unnamed) psychic healer, at the University of Chile, produced a significant retardation of tumor growth in mice injected with malignant tissue, as compared with control groups not treated by the healer.

As already noted, these and other experiments, fully monitored and officially reported, are *proof* of the psychic healer's powers. But what they also show is that it is not the case that the healer somehow "persuades" his human patients into triggering their *own* autonomic system to deal with their wounds and illnesses. You can't "persuade" mice to heal their own wounds! This is quite clear, absolutely clear: the healer emits some sort of healing energy.

So here, then, is a matter of *major* significance—one, of course, as with all our other material, almost totally ignored by the scientific and academic establishments—and our university courses, textbooks, and the like.

We have already mentioned the condition of multiple personality.

And we should stress once again that this is a (neurotic) condition that affects *women* far more than *men*.

In this condition, a fully integrated alternative personality, and often several such personalities, takes over and displaces the individual's normal conscious self—often for weeks and months at a time. During this time, the normal self disappears completely—and when it returns, it has no memory whatsoever of the missing period of time or any of its events, nor of the alternative personality itself.

This is no matter of play-acting. The alternative personality has different beliefs, views, ideals, temperament, ambitions, tastes, habits, experiences, and memories—and different health, different voice, different facial expressions, and so forth—from the normal owner of the body (and also from the other alternative personalities, if more than one is involved). But more importantly and crucially still, the new personality shows *different brain-wave patterns* (electroencephalograms) and produces different handwriting, different performances on word-association and other formal tests. In particular here, it must be stressed that in no way whatsoever can ordinary individuals consciously or deliberately change their brain-wave patterns without special intensive training.

Excellent detail in these matters is given in the book *The Three Faces of Eve* by C. H. Thigpen and H. M. Checkley. Eve White had been referred to a psychiatrist. She and her husband were both deeply religious (but of different faiths). Their sex life was unsatisfactory, and they had disputes about the upbringing of their child. Eve had begun to suffer from blinding headaches and occasional mental blackouts.

During a year of psychotherapy, there was actually a worsening of her general condition—she would purchase items and then completely forget that she had bought them, she began to hear disembodied voices, and so on. Then, abruptly, during a psychotherapy session, the first of her alternative personalities appeared. These are the words of the doctors involved:

The brooding look in her eyes became almost a stare. Suddenly her posture began to change. Her body slowly stiffened until she sat rigidly erect. An alien, inexplicable expression then came over her face. This was suddenly erased into utter blankness. The lines of her countenance seemed to shift in a barely visible, slow rippling transformation. For a moment there was the impression of something arcane. Closing her eyes, she winced as she put her hands to her temples, pressed hard and twisted them as if to combat sudden pain. A slight shudder passed over her entire body.

Then the hands lightly dropped. She relaxed easily into an attitude of comfort the physician had never before seen in this patient. A pair of blue eyes popped open. There was a quick reckless smile. In a bright unfamiliar voice that sparkled, the woman said 'Hi there, Doc!'

With a soft and surprisingly intimate syllable of laughter, she crossed her legs, carelessly swirling her skirt in the process. She unhurriedly smoothed the hem down over her knees in a manner that was playful and somehow just a little provocative. From a corner of his preoccupied awareness the physician had vaguely noted for the first time how attractive these legs were. She settled a little more deeply into the cushions of the chair. The demure and constrained posture of Eve White had melted into buoyant repose. One little foot crossed over the other began a low, small, rhythmic, rocking motion that seemed to express contentment as pervasively as the gentle wagging of a fox-terrier's tail.

A third personality later emerged—quite unlike the other two. Apart from dramatic psychological differences, the authors note that this third person even seemed taller when standing than the other two! She also had command of languages that far exceeded that of the two others. (Sadly, Eve White later had a full mental breakdown. In the course of this, twenty different personalities manifested themselves.)

A point perhaps to stress is the suddenness—the space of a few seconds—with which the alternative personality manifests itself, with its different physical and mental attributes.

Absolutely remarkable though all the events of this chapter are, they do not appear to violate the laws of normal, that is, our objective time and space. But the events of the next chapter go further still—they do break the laws of time and space (yet more torment for our half-brained scientists!).

In conclusion here—impulses from the two cerebral hemispheres cross to the *opposite* cerebellar hemispheres, and vice-versa. So, vis-à-vis the cerebrum, the cerebellum is left-handed (like our own image in a mirror).

Now we know for a fact that neither of the cerebral hemispheres alone produces handedness—because when either of the cerebral hemispheres is removed by surgery, the patient shows no change of handedness. So is it a strong cerebellum that is responsible for left-handedness? If that were shown to be the case, this would of course provide convincing support for my claim that Neanderthals were left-handed.

Chapter 10
Proof of Psychic Abilities in Humans and Animals

TELEPATHY IS A FACT. A *fact*. Minds, both human and animal, can communicate naturally with each other, no matter how far separated they are. Distance apart seems to have no effect, no weakening effect, whatsoever.

We have countless instances of the above, and two examples are described in detail below. These involve numerous reliable, professional people, including vets. Some of the accounts have been published in reputable magazines and journals, such as the *New Scientist,* They are, collectively never mind singly, *proof* of the reality of telepathy.

A professional engineer, Grindle Matthews, had gone on a business trip to New York. He had left his cat in the care of his housekeeper. The cat had been partially paralyzed after an accident as a youngster. One night, the engineer woke from a nightmare. He had seen his cat struggling in the hands of a man wearing a white coat and with a goatee beard. The hotel room seemed to the inventor to smell of chloroform. Next day, he telegraphed home asking about the cat, but received no reply.

When he eventually went home, he learned that his cat had refused to eat in his absence. The housekeeper had been unable to stand the sight of the paralyzed cat starving to death. But instead of contacting her employer, as of course she should have done, the housekeeper called in a vet and had the cat put to sleep. The vet had a goatee beard. The time of the cat's death coincided with Matthew's nightmare.

Osbert Hewitt was visiting friends in London. His cat, Mitzi, was left at home in Oxford. That night, Hewitt dreamed that his cat, dressed as a volunteer in the Spanish Civil War, had come to him badly wounded, begging and pleading for his help. He tried to reassure the cat, promising to take her to the hospital. But Mitzi continued screaming. Hewitt woke very disturbed and checked the time. It was 4:00 a.m. He told his hostess of this strange nightmare next morning. After he then left the house, the telephone rang. It was Hewitt's housekeeper, reporting that Mitzi had been badly injured in a fight the previous night. The cat had been found howling on Hewitt's pillow at 4:00 a.m., after waking the whole household.

The psychologist Dr. Martin Schatzman had a patient named Ruth, who had a history of vivid hallucinations, which often conveyed real information paranormally. Dr. Schatzman asked Ruth in one of her therapy sessions if she would now hallucinate a figure and talk to it. At this point, Ruth's grandmother appeared to her. Ruth's grandmother said that she was waiting for Ruth at home. (But Ruth lived in London, and her grandmother in America.) The apparition then said: "No matter what happens, you'll always have me. I don't want you to worry that you won't." So Ruth asked, "'Will I ever see you? Will you be dead when I get there?" The grandmother said: "I'll only be as dead as you'll let me be." As she spoke these words, the hallucination of the grandmother had tears running down her face, but was smiling. The incident occurred at 4:30 p.m. London time. Ruth's grandmother, who was still in America, died there unexpectedly, six and a half hours later.

Mrs. Terris, the wife of the actor-manager of the Adelphi Theatre in London, was at home in the living room of her house. Her two sons were playing chess. The family's fox terrier, Davie, was asleep in her lap. At 7:20 p.m., abruptly and without warning, Davie leaped from Mrs. Terris's lap and began dashing frantically around the room, yelping and snapping, in a paroxysm of rage and fear. The dog seemed to be looking at something. "What does he see?" asked Mrs. Terris. So odd was the dog's behavior, all the family were upset for the rest of the evening.

Just after 7:00 p.m. on that December evening, William Terris, actor-manager of the Adelphi Theatre in London, was about to open the door of his private entrance at the back of the theater when a man called William Prince, an actor who believed that Terris was blocking his career, sprang out from the shadows and stabbed Terris twice with a dagger. The shouts alerted passers-by, and Terris was carried into the theater. He died twenty minutes later.

In a case reported in a journal by J. G. Pratt, the pet dog of a family in New Jersey suddenly went under the house and began continually whining and crying. It had never behaved like this before. The family was unable to persuade the dog to come out or to stop his whining and "strange barking." Later that day came the news that the elder son of the family had been killed in a car accident on the way home from college. The times of the accident and the onset of the dog's behavior were identical.

The following incident was reported by a vet. A dog was staying with the vet while his family was on holiday. At 10:00 a.m. one morning, the dog began howling and barking in an alarming fashion. Then, after an hour or so, the behavior abruptly stopped. It was the only time during his stay that the dog had displayed this behavior. The vet examined the dog carefully but could find nothing wrong with him. When the family returned, the vet told them of the incident. They reported, in astonishment, that at ten o'clock on the morning in question, they had been trapped on top of their car in a flash flood. They were rescued an hour later, around eleven.

An American sergeant in Vietnam had surprise leave and arrived home on a Thursday without prior notice. But early on Wednesday, his dog, Nellie, had frenziedly dashed upstairs, jumped all over the sergeant's bed, brought down his slippers to the living room, and then taken up a post at the front door, refusing to budge until Sergeant Johnson "unexpectedly" (!) came home through the door the next day.

David Fitzgerald, an estate agent in Ireland, had a son in Australia called Freddy. One night in Ireland, Fitzgerald was awakened by the howling of the spaniel, which was the family dog of their son Freddy. Fitzgerald woke his wife and said he felt sure there was something wrong with Freddy. Later again he woke her, shouting, "I saw Freddy, I saw Freddy! He was at the bottom of the bed looking at me." The next day's post brought a letter with the news of son Freddy's unexpected death.

May we mention in passing here that knowledge of the death of a member of the tribe, currently away from the tribe, is absolutely commonplace among Australian aborigines? *Absolutely commonplace.*

There are many reports of strong telepathic communication between mothers and preschool children—which, however, is subsequently lost.

For example, a social psychologist was sitting watching her small daughter and another little girl playing weddings with their dolls. The mother herself was wondering whether to go and see the film *Blood Wedding* that afternoon. Then, to her astonishment, she heard her daughter announce: "This isn't a church wedding, it's a blood wedding."

There are also many, many reports of pets (dogs, cats, horses, birds, and so forth) separated from their owners by some set of circumstances—being lost on holiday, stolen, sold, or whatever—who subsequently find their way across hundreds, sometimes *thousands* of miles of unknown territory to be reunited with their owners. These pets *know* where their owners are—like the howling dogs and meowing cats described before, they have *constant* mental contact with the ones they love (as do, of course, some owners with their pets), and distance is no object whatsoever.

A famous case is that of a dog called Bobbie. He was lost by an American family while they were in Wolcott, Indiana, on August 6, 1923. The dog reappeared at his home in Silverton, Oregon, six months later, on February 15, 1924. The distance involved is 3,000 miles as the crow flies. Bobbie's condition showed that the dog had suffered very considerable hardship—the intervening months had of course been winter. The owners now placed advertisements in various newspapers to try to establish whether anyone recalled seeing or feeding the dog en route. Several people came forward. They testified that they had fed and temporarily housed Bobbie in his pathetic condition. He stayed with the various owners for a few days before gathering strength. But as soon as he was well enough to walk again and his paws had healed, he set off once again.

Here is another remarkable case. During the First World War, James Brown went from Britain to France with his regiment. Two months later his dog, who had pined badly since his owner's departure, disappeared from Brown's London house. A fortnight after that, the dog ran up to James in the trenches at Armentiers in France.

James' dog had "hitchhiked" his way across the Channel—and we have plenty of hard evidence of such hitchhiking.

A ship sailed away from Australia on November 22, leaving behind the ship's cat. But on January 20, the cat walked aboard the ship in the London docks.

In another instance, Captain Kenneth Dodson of the United States Navy published a book titled *Hector the Stowaway Dog*. Hector (who had gone missing from his own ship) was first observed walking about on four different ships in the docks in Vancouver by a ship's officer, H. Kildall. After watching the dog for a while, Kildall went about his duties. And now his own ship, the SS *Hanley*, sailed off. But the next morning on the ship, Kildall was confronted with Hector. The dog was looked after but refused to make friends with any of the crew. But as the *Hanley* eventually approached the coast of Japan, the dog's studied indifference was replaced with excitement. The *Hanley* now dropped anchor in Yokohama. The nearest other ship, a Dutch vessel, was anchored 300 yards away—but Hector was watching it in excitement. A rowing boat now put out from the Dutch ship and passed the *Hanley*. Hector jumped into the water and swam up to the rowing boat. In it was Hector's owner.

As noted, we have *hundreds* of cases of this kind confirmed by many witnesses, and other hard evidence. So, as ever, we are talking *facts* here.

We will get to my own direct involvement in these kinds of matters later. But let me state at this point that I have conclusively demonstrated my own ability to communicate telepathically on British national television.

I was invited to appear on an afternoon chat show by Granada TV in the 1980s. During our discussion before the show started, the presenter asked me if I could place an image telepathically in the minds of the viewers. I said yes, I could, and would.

So, during the show I transmitted the image—which was a triangle enclosed in a circle. The switchboards in Manchester and Liverpool were jammed for the rest of the day by viewers calling in to say they had seen the image. Hardly one they could have invented for themselves, is it?

Only one member of the small studio audience got the image (well, almost)—but then, I was not focusing on them. Before the program, the studio audience had been given pieces of paper and pencils

Figure 10.1. The image transmitted.

Figure 10.2. The image received by a member of the studio audience.

so they could draw the image. They handed in their drawings before I announced what my image had been. One young man had drawn a capital A in a circle.

But that can hardly be any kind of coincidence.

We turn now to the matter of seeing the future (and also seeing the unknown past.)

A television producer had a dream, in color. In the dream, he was watching a race on television. The commentator of the race grew very excited. Three horses were neck and neck as they approached the finish line. The names of the three horses were repeated several times. The winner of the close finish was an outsider, not expected to win.

We should stress at this point that the producer had no interest whatsoever in gambling. The name of the winning horse hovered in the mind of the producer for several days. (That is already a little unusual, since usually we forget dream material very rapidly.) But he attached no importance to the dream as a whole. However, in the course of the next day or so, the producer realized that a former acquaintance of his had once had a share in a horse of that name. So he called his former acquaintance. The man said that the horse had never looked as if it would do well, so he had sold his share. But he did know that the horse was due to run again soon.

The producer looked through the racing pages for several days and eventually found the race in which the horse was running. Now he saw the other two horses named in his dream were also running. Greatly impressed by this "coincidence," he placed a "very large" (we are not told the actual amount) sum of money on his dream horse.

But very importantly, from the evidentiary point of view, he told all his staff and colleagues the details of the situation so far, and he suggested that they all sit and watch the race on television, which they did. The race finished *exactly* as described in the dream. The three named horses fought out the closely contested finish, and the producer's horse won (at 22:1 odds)!

Another woman, an educational psychologist—again a woman with no interest whatsoever in gambling—dreamed the winners of races three or four times a week *for four months*. Her dreams were vivid and in color. The names of the winning horses were announced clearly by the commentator in the dreams. At this point, the woman began telling her husband about the dreams—and he began searching for the named horses in the papers and placing bets on them. The horses named won each time, and the husband significantly increased the bets. He now had enough to buy a new car, and did so. At this point the dreams abruptly ceased.

Another woman, a devout Catholic, began dreaming the winners of horse races. The dreams were without sound, but she clearly saw the number of the horse as it crossed the line. She told her husband of these dreams, and he began looking for the winning horse's number each day—and each day duly produced the winner. But the couple placed no bets because of their religious beliefs. Nevertheless, the woman woke one morning and told her husband that the two horses she had dreamed about that night would produce £1,000 (about $2,000) for a small bet known as the Tote Double. They decided to buy a Tote ticket and to give the money to charity. Both the horses duly won, and the Tote Double that day paid £964.

As a boy, Lewis Thompson, the brother of the writer Martin Thompson, could tell the winners of horse races by looking over the horses in the paddock. He said that the horses "talked to him" in his head. Quite apart from his substantial success in picking winners in this way, he also sometimes obtained other information. Once he told an owner that *that* horse would win (it was an outsider, unlikely to do so); and that another horse—a strongly fancied favorite—was lame. His remarks caused some amusement, because the fancied horse was perfectly sound. But in the *actual* race, the 22:1 outsider the boy had chosen did win, while the fancied favorite pulled up lame.

As a keen gambler myself, I regret that I can report one occasion of myself dreaming a racehorse winner. I had the same dream twice in one night. In it, a group of us were in line outside a movie theater to see a film, the name of which was not known. We got into the theater, and the film began—then the first dream ended. In the second version of the dream, the film began—in color this time—and its name was announced—"Showman's Fair." The film ended very quickly, and the plot was unclear, yet afterward, all agreed it had been very exciting.

Next day, I was surprised to see that a horse was running called Showman's Fair—I had no memory of seeing that horse's name before. It was an elderly horse, eleven years old, with no recent form. I placed £5 on it to win (the equivalent of that today would be more like £20)—and fortunately, I told the whole story to a business and sports journalist (Roy Grant) before the race began. The horse duly won at 7:2.

Let me give here one more instance of myself dreaming the future.

In this dream I was standing next to and talking to Isaac Asimov (a man I had never actually met, although I am a great admirer of his books). When I say "talking," we were, in fact, not talking at all. I was desperately racking my brains to think of something he had written in order to begin a conversation. I knew we were at a party, though in fact no one else was present. Indeed, he and I were floating in a gray mist suspended in space. It was the fact that we were each holding a drink that made me feel it was a party. I noticed that Asimov was taller than me, though I do not know if he actually was. (If so, he would have had to be around six feet.) That was the dream, and this was a Wednesday night.

A few days earlier, I had written a letter to the *New Scientist*. The chances of getting a letter published in a major journal are, of course, always small—they get such a volume of mail.

But, in fact, the next day's *New Scientist* (Thursday) carried my letter. In the column next to it was a letter from Isaac Asimov. His letter was longer than mine.

So there we were "standing next to each other," and he was indeed "taller" than me.

The "gray mist," I think, represented the printed page, and the other letters were the "party." And guess what—my own letter was about dreaming! His letter was on a totally different subject—so we had nothing to say to each other.

Let's enrage the mainstream scientific community even further.

It is the case—and we have clear experiential evidence on this matter—that animals can also see/sense the future. We have, of course, a clear nudge about this in the case of the "hitchhiking" animals we looked at earlier. That they know where their master or mistress *is,* is one thing. But how, for instance, did Hector know that the ship he stowed away on was bound for Japan? As we know, the dog had already been seen on four ships in those docks. But the one he *chose,* the fifth one, took him to his owner. The same comment applies to the other animals involved. How did they know the vessel they chose was going where they needed to go?

So, a girl was playing with her younger two-year-old brother and their dog in the living room of their home. The little boy fell over, cried, and was comforted. The tiny incident was forgotten. But that evening, the family noticed that the child was using his left hand to eat instead of his right. They massaged the child's right arm, but there seemed to be nothing wrong with it. Then the dog suddenly approached the child's chair and began howling in a very odd and disturbed way. They put the dog in the next room, but the howling continued, so they put him out in the garden. The dog now took up a position under the child's window and continued his noise all evening, despite repeated attempts to quiet him and drive him away from the house. The boy died at one o'clock next morning. Outside, the dog fell silent.

A woman's husband had been an invalid for some time, but on this particular day he seemed no different from usual. On that day, the dog suddenly squeezed herself under an armchair and began whining pitifully and continuously. "What the devil's the matter with the dog?" said the husband. "Anyone would think she was announcing my death." On the following day, the man died.

Many of the cases we are looking at also involve the "suicide" of the pet concerned.

An old farmer and his dog were inseparable companions. One morning, the old man announced from his bed that he would not be getting up any more and that he was dying. The son told his father he was talking nonsense. But the old man was adamant and asked for his dog to be brought up so he could say good-bye to him. The irritated son brought up the dog. He jumped on the bed and nuzzled the old man affectionately—but then abruptly retreated into the corner, howling and showing the whites of his eyes. The dog was taken down to his kennel, petted, and offered food—but it would not stop howling. The dog died that evening at 9.30 p.m. The farmer died at 10:00 p.m.

A British police sergeant had a slight accident while cycling on his rounds. A little shaken, he returned home. As he stepped across the threshold, his dog, Tim, began running wildly about the house, staring fixedly at nothing. But he did not bark, and, in fact, never barked again. The sergeant now went up to bed to rest. At first his few grazes from the accident gave him no cause for concern. But his general condition grew steadily worse. The dog now lay permanently under the bed and refused to eat or drink. As the sergeant's illness seriously progressed, the dog developed identical symptoms—blindness and paralysis of the limbs. The dog's symptoms were officially confirmed by a vet who came to examine the dog. The police sergeant died in his bed a few days later. The dog died at the same moment.

Let's move on to *actual experiments* with animals.

Mice were put, singly, into a box from which they could move to any of a number of adjoining boxes. Once in the new box, they were not allowed to return. After a large number of mice had made their individual choices, each choice was randomly correlated on a computer, with the two judgments, "correct" and "incorrect." The mice that were assigned the judgment "incorrect" were then painlessly put to death.

As the experiment proceeded, notes had been kept of the sex, size, weight, color, and other physical characteristics of the mice who successfully avoided the random selection for death. Now new mice were selected possessing these characteristics. The new mice were subjected to the same earlier experimental procedure. The new mice evaded death at a rate *far in excess of chance.*

Rats become less active when threatened with danger. One experiment studied a group of rats and ranked them on their activity level. A second experimenter (who had no contact with the first experimenter) then activated a computer procedure that randomly decided that certain of the rats should be put to death. Subsequent examination showed that those rats put to death had shown *significantly lower values of activity than those left alive.* Yet when the activity levels were rated, the random decisions concerning death had not even been taken.

A similar experiment involved goldfish. Unlike rats, goldfish became *more* active when threatened with danger. The goldfish were given a long series of trials. Each was given an activity rating during a short period, before a random process decided which goldfish should be lifted out of the water—a very disturbing event for a goldfish. The series produced *significant* correlations between high activity and the subsequent lifting out of the water.

One more example. This experiment was stylishly ingenious. It was totally automated, so no experimenter had any idea what was happening until the results were in.

Mice were kept in a cage uniform in all respects, except that it was divided by a partition into two parts over which the mice could easily climb. The random procedure was that an electric shock was passed through one side of the floor (made of copper) or the other on a random basis. Two kinds of event were recorded: (1) when a mouse moved from a side where it had not been shocked to the side where it would now receive a shock; and (2) more importantly, when a mouse moved back to the side on which it had last been shocked. Yet whichever of these moves a mouse chose, this could, in normal terms, in *no way* make a difference to the number of times it was shocked. The mouse *could not* avoid or defeat the number of times it was shocked by any normal process of choice or lack of choice. Nothing it could decide to do, either by strategy or randomly, could reduce or change over a period the number of times it was shocked. (Is that clear?)

But, in fact, the mice avoided shock *at a very high level of significance*. In 612 trials, they avoided shock on average 53 times more than they should have.

(What, sir/madam, you haven't heard of or read about *any* of this material? *How come* that is?)

So the ability of animals, never mind human beings, to paranormally anticipate the future is *proven beyond all argument or debate*.

We will mention only in passing here paranormal perception of the past—that is, of information known to no living person, such as the whereabouts of a will or testament.

Much more amazingly, "psychic archaeologists" can detect the presence of concealed remains of ancient civilizations of which there is no sign whatsoever on the surface, sometimes in astonishing detail. Here is just a brief extract from Geoffrey Goodman's book *Psychic Archaeology:*

> The digging so far consists of twenty-eight foot deep exploratory shaft. Not only was the psychic amazingly accurate in locating this new deep site which had no surface indications to recommend it—a site most archaeology professors said couldn't possibly exist—but the psychic was also amazingly accurate in the geological, chronological and archaeological details he predicted we would encounter in our digging. Crude stone tools have been recovered throughout the shaft as predicted: changes in geology have occurred at the exact depths predicted and radiocarbon dating proves the very early dates predicted. Of the fifty-eight specific predictions tested so far, fifty-one have proved correct. That is eighty-seven percent accuracy.

So with regard to psychic ability to see the unknown past, we are talking *fact*. Fact, fact, fact, fact, fact.

Precisely the same is true of the phenomenon known as poltergeist activity (and, of course, of all the material of this second part of the book). Poltergeist activity is where objects move and noises are produced without any normal influence being involved. (An instance in which I was personally concerned will be mentioned later.)

We have many, many authenticated cases on record. The events briefly described here were witnessed and confirmed by the Reverend T. W. Lund, Dr. W. H. Nisbett, M.B., Ch.B., Dr. William Logan, M.B., Ch.B., Dr. Sheila Logan, M.B., Ch.B, DPH (the wife of William Logan), Mrs. Margaret Stewart (Virginia's schoolteacher), and also other witnesses.* The case was specifically investigated by Prof. A. R. G. Owen, fellow of mathematics and lecturer in genetics at Cambridge University. This was in 1961. As Owen points out, the witnesses are not only people with integrity, but trained observers. Their courage in speaking out must also be endorsed—for, of course, they risk damaging their professional reputations and careers.

The source of the many phenomena was Virginia Campbell, an eleven-year-old girl going through puberty. She had spells of falling into trance, when she would talk and call out. For this she was being treated by Dr. Nisbett. Some of the many events observed by Dr. Nisbett are these: Mr. and Mrs. Campbell, Virginia's mother and father, saw a large linen chest (measuring 27 × 17 × 14 inches) full of bed linens raise itself from the floor and move some eighteen inches across the floor before moving back to its original position. At the same time, there was an outburst of paranormal knocking.

At school in the classroom, Mrs. Stewart saw a desk behind Virginia rise slowly from the floor, then settle gently down again. Meanwhile, Virginia was trying to hold down the lid of her own desk, which was forcing itself open.

Dr. Nisbett, sitting in the bedroom while Virginia went to sleep,

---

*Ch.B. stands for Bachelor of Surgery and M.B. is Bachelor of Medicine; both are equivalent to the U.S. M.D. degree. DPH is Doctor of Public Health.

heard outbursts of knocking. Then the linen chest already mentioned moved about a foot. The lid of the chest opened and shut itself several times. Virginia's pillow began rotating, and the ripples ran through the bedclothes.

Nisbett had already observed the pillow rotating and the rippling effect on a previous occasion, and also heard knockings and sawing noises. He now stayed in the bedroom on several occasions while Virginia went to sleep. He found that the sequence of events was always the same—the rippling effect on the bedclothes, then noise, then movement of the chest. On one occasion, before the chest was due to move itself, Nisbett moved it to the other side of the bedroom. But still the chest's lid opened itself several times.

On a subsequent occasion, the events described were *also* confirmed by Dr. Logan.

At school also, the events continued. While Virginia was standing next to the teacher's table, a board pointer on it began to vibrate, then moved and fell to the floor. Mrs. Stewart put her hand on the table and felt it begin to vibrate. Then the table itself began to move, swinging in a circular motion away from the teacher and Virginia. Again, on a subsequent occasion, a bowl of flowers moved itself across the table.

Virginia was at one point taken away to stay in another town. Here, once again, the paranormal bangings and knockings were repeated. But now Virginia fell into a trance and began speaking in an unnatural voice. (So she was beginning to behave like a medium.)

Back home again, an apple floated out of a bowl, and a shaving brush flew around the room. Two visiting little girls were poked, pinched, and nipped by unseen forces, as was also a home visitor. On three occasions, Mrs. Campbell saw Virginia's lips turn a bright red. And so on and so on.

There are many other cases we could cite. Here we will mention just one more brief incident.

The well-known analysts Sigmund Freud and Carl Jung were sitting discussing the paranormal. Freud, who always vehemently rejected what he called "the black tide of mud of occultism," made an insulting remark concerning Jung's support of the paranormal. Jung was very angry at this totally unjustified snub, but bit back his anger. But then as Jung himself reports,

> Now I had a curious sensation. It was as if my diaphragm were made of iron and was becoming red hot—a glowing vault. And at that moment there was such a loud report in the bookcase which stood right next to us, that we both started up in alarm, fearing the bookcase was going to topple over on us. I said to Freud, "there is an example of a so-called exteriorisation phenomenon."
>
> "Oh come," he exclaimed. "That is sheer bosh."
>
> "It is not." I replied. "You are mistaken, Herr Professor. And to prove my point I now predict that in a moment there will be another loud report."
>
> Sure enough, no sooner had I said the words than the same detonation went off in the bookcase.
>
> To this day I do not know what gave me this certainty. But I knew beyond any all doubt that the report would come again. Freud only stared aghast at me.

We turn now to the matter of spontaneous combustion. This is an extremely important phenomenon for two reasons (apart, that is, from its own complete amazingness).

1. Scientists do not dispute its existence. How could they? How could they dispute the findings of *hundreds* of coroner's inquests, and medical and police investigations?
2. *Far more women* are involved in it than men—just as is the case, of course, with dreaming, multiple personality, automatic writing, the production of spontaneous wounds on the body, psychic-telepathic visions, mediumship (and more women are *outstanding* mediums), poltergeist phenomena, neurosis, and so

on and on for all the items we are examining. (And, of course—
and we cannot say this too often—women have a larger cerebellum than men, with a considerably different structure.)

What occurs in spontaneous human combustion is that the body
suddenly—often in the space of a few minutes—is totally consumed
by an *intense* internal fire. In this the flesh, organs, and bones of the
individual are reduced to a heap of ashes. A staggering temperature in
excess of 3,000 degrees is required to burn bones. Yet this *incredible*
heat sometimes leaves the victim's clothes only slightly charred. A chair
that the victim has been sitting on may be untouched. No surrounding
fire is started by any victim—the immense heat is somehow contained,
and miraculously so. And a person can suffer spontaneous human combustion while walking down a street, or, in one case, while dancing in a
ballroom with a boyfriend—so in full view of onlookers.

There is no explanation whatsoever for this utterly amazing event.
And as already stated, it is fully authentic and authenticated. There is no
dispute whatsoever by orthodoxy concerning its existence and reality.

But we can note here that bursts of paranormal fire sometimes
accompany poltergeist events. (And maybe Jung was lucky not to spontaneously combust during his argument with Freud!)

This is perhaps the moment to begin to talk about my own per-
sonal involvement in the matters we have been discussing.

In my early twenties, after obtaining a degree in modern languages
in London, I went to Birmingham (not Coventry, as stated in earlier
books to preserve the privacy of certain individuals) to work as a substitute teacher in general subjects, wondering what to do with my life. I
joined a beginner's course in gymnastics—because I had to teach gymnastics in my own class. At the gym in the changing room, I got to
know a young man called Brian. He was in the advanced class. (He
later told me that his spirit guide had instructed him to talk to me.)
Brian was a psychic medium. And he is an instructive example to those
who think psychics are necessarily oddball weirdos—for he was very

good at and very interested in gymnastics. When we got to know each other better, Brian asked if I would like to come to a séance, to which I said yes.

A full account of the events of this, my first psychic experience, is given in appendix 2.

Here we will just note that during that first séance, I suddenly felt a rush of energy from the back of my head—I can't say it was from the cerebellum; I had never heard of the cerebellum—and I fell into an unconscious trance.

Apparently, during this period of unconsciousness, several "spirits" spoke through me, as the other members of the group subsequently told me. The medium leading the group said that I was a gifted psychic and invited me to join a regular group of mediums (of whom Brian was one) working to develop their gifts. And so once or twice a week from then on, I attended the group.

At these meetings, various "spirits" would possess one or other of the group (all of whom, of course, were psychics). It might be the "spirit" of a person, say, who had been killed in a car accident, or had committed suicide, and who now wandered in limbo, not even understanding that they were dead. These "spirits" would then be given advice and counseling.

But far more remarkable (as far as I was and am concerned) was that in this small sitting room, only faintly lit by a shielded electric light, we would all experience collective hallucinations. Sometimes, the room would be filled with a bright, shining luminosity. Sometimes we would see (collectively) the figure of the dead "spirit" walking or standing in the room. I never said (first) what I saw. I waited until the others gave their descriptions of what they had seen.

One instance impressed me quite strongly at the time—but far more strongly later, for obvious reasons. On this occasion we saw, standing in the corner of the room and breathing nervously, the figure of a caveman—a stocky, rather bulky individual, covered with hair and wearing some kind of bear pelt. The figure did not say anything, even though the presiding medium gently asked what it wanted, and whether we could help it in any way. But it just stood, breathing nervously, and then faded.

In those days, I had barely heard of the Neanderthals. But that is what this figure was. This experience was, clearly and absolutely, a paranormal vision of my own future concerns. (I wish I could say that the figure had had red hair! But no. It was middle-aged, and had grayish-brown hair.)

As regards my own trance conditions, I had now learned to remain conscious when the "spirit" took me over. It is a remarkable experience to be possessed by a "spirit" (the quotation marks are deliberate, incidentally). One's normal consciousness stands to one side, so to speak. And it is as if someone is putting on your body, is dressing themselves in your body. Your hands, for example, become old and gnarled. Your back stoops. You become nearsighted, and you are now an elderly person, perhaps breathing with difficulty. When you speak, it is in the voice of another person.

I do not believe, and have never believed, that these "spirits" are the souls or minds of departed individuals who once lived. They are creations and products of our own "other mind." (I am going to dump the term *unconscious mind* from now on.) As in the case of dreams, as in the case of multiple personality, as in the case of hypnosis, as in the case of regression back to childhood, and so on. (Thus, for example, we have instances of families who go to visit a medium to contact a dead member of the family, and the dead individual speaks to them through the medium. But, in fact, the individual concerned is *not* dead at all but is only *believed* to be dead by the misinformed family. Therefore, there would not be a "departed spirit" to speak to and any communication would be a product of the mind.)

One further item here. I was sitting with Brian in his house, and we were discussing psychic phenomena. At this point, a book suddenly flew off the table in front of me and landed on the floor. Brian smiled at my look of disbelief. (This incident is a remarkable parallel to what took place between Freud and Jung, as cited earlier. But I was not *denying* poltergeist phenomena. I was merely saying I had never witnessed such an event.)

After some six months of the mediumistic group sessions, I returned to London. But clearly, my life had changed. I was now on a full mission of exploration. I enrolled for a course at the College of Psychic Studies in London. But I also decided to take a degree course in psychology (at Birkbeck College), and as well to have a full (Jungian) psychoanalysis.

Details of my subsequent career as a professional psychologist have already been given in an earlier chapter.

But my contact with the "psychic world" was now permanent.

One more example of that (some have already been given earlier). I was traveling home from work on a London Underground train, a journey I made every day. I was not reading a book or a newspaper, nor was I in any way preoccupied. We reached my home station (as I thought), and I got off the train. The ascending escalator was empty, apart from myself and an elderly man several steps above me. When the man reached the top of the escalator, he suddenly staggered and fell backward. I was able to catch him as he fell—otherwise he would certainly have suffered (serious) injury.

Then it was not until we both stepped off the escalator at the top that I suddenly realized I was at the wrong station—the one before my own stop. Yes, of course there are major differences between the two stations. I had been in some kind of (precognitive) trance state.

Let us now make some very emphatic statements in conclusion.

The distinguished scientist/inventor/philosopher/theologian Emmanuel Swedenborg stated unequivocally that trance and mystical inspiration arise and derive from the cerebellum. The cerebellum is, he said, the source of wisdom, the source of visionary powers—that "angels speak to us" through the cerebellum.

Swedenborg's own psychic abilities are well documented. For example, a widow was being pursued for a considerable debt, which she claimed her late husband had already paid. She went to Swedenborg for his help. He told her that the receipt was hidden in a secret panel behind her husband's desk—of which the woman herself had no knowledge. The receipt was duly found behind the panel Swedenborg had described.

Jerome Cardan, a British royal physician, also unequivocally states that trance begins in the cerebellum and is the source of paranormal powers—as do many other less-well-known individuals.

But a further important point to consider is that Swedenborg and Cardan—along with Marcel Vogel, senior chemist, mentioned earlier, and also myself—so four of us altogether—are *proof* that it is perfectly possible to have an outstanding academic/scientific/medical career, whatever—one that is fully acknowledged by other members of the professions—and yet be totally committed to the veracity, the reality, and the importance of the psychic world, of the "alternative universe." And *also* to have the *actual ability* to employ its paranormal powers.

The blatant (and pathetic) denial of the alternative universe and its many features has been well noted by others apart from myself.

> The modern physicist experiences the world through extreme specialization of the rational mind; the mystic through an extreme specialization of the intuitive mind. The two approaches are entirely different and involve far more than a certain view of the physical world. . . . Neither is comprehended in the other, nor can either of them be reduced to the other. . . . Science does not need mysticism and mysticism does not need science; but man needs both.
>
> FRITJOF CAPRA

> But the sceptics are happier in their singleness and simplicity, happy that they do not, will not, realize the monstrous events that lie only just beneath the surface.
>
> MONTAGUE SUMMERS

We live in a truly dark cage, lit only here and there by a few candles.

MARLYN PRYER

Modern man is as fanatic in his non-belief as ancient man had been in his faith.

HERMAN GOMBINER

Our next chapter specifically supports the view expressed by Fritjof Capra.

Chapter 11

Two Brains— and Two Universes

AS WE HAVE ALREADY clearly seen, and as is independently confirmed by a variety of thinkers, it is the case that we inhabit "two universes" (which turns out to be rather more than mere metaphor).

And that we are each of us "in two minds." This particular situation is further confirmed by psychoanalysts' division of the mind into the unconscious and the conscious, into the Self and the Ego.

There are two reasons for our "two minds" duality.

1. As set out in part 1, we, modern humans, are a hybrid cross between two varieties of early human, Neanderthal and Cro-Magnon. And as is common when two widely separated species cross, the offspring frequently inherit and exhibit two sets of opposing instincts, a situation with which they struggle to come to terms.

2. But much more importantly still, we each of us have *two brains*— two highly evolved and complex brains—the cerebrum and the cerebellum. As already described and detailed, these two brains function differently and in many ways separately from each other—though by no means completely.

The above two items are themselves also interlinked. That is, the Neanderthal had a much larger cerebellum than the Cro-Magnon. And a further relevant point, of course, is that women have a much larger cerebellum than men—one that is very differently structured.

Yet, as already stated, you will search our university textbooks (as well as your television screen and newspapers) for *any* mention of these matters and their very, very important consequences. That is, their absolutely *crucial* consequences.

Item (1) above is the reason why we have, through the whole of human society worldwide, *two* diametrically opposed political positions, two opposed political parties—the left wing (communism, socialism, democrats) and the right wing (fascism, conservatism, republicanism).

But, as noted, no one *ever* asks why these two situations exist!

If lions, horses, bears, dogs, whatever, evolved into highly intelligent beings, there would quite certainly in each case be just one society (one world)—the lion society. The horse society. The bear society. The dog society.

But *we* have effectively two societies (two worlds) in one—the Neanderthal society and the Cro-Magnon society.

As already stated, the Cro-Magnon society champions marriage (that is, pair-bonding), leadership by males, the stiff upper lip, efficiency, rank order—all of what are *today* often described as "old-fashioned" values. Whereas the nowadays ever-more-powerful Neanderthal scenario is basically anti-marriage, pro-feminist, pro-gay, soft on crime, soft on cheating, inefficient, in favor of equality for all, and so on.

But of much greater consequence still is item (2) above, the fact that each of us has *two* highly evolved brains.

It is this basic duality of our being that I claim produces these fundamental pairs: religion/science; neurosis/psychosis; dreaming/waking; subjectivity/objectivity; faith/proof; emotion/thought—and so on and so on.

We have so far not mentioned the detail and the difference between the two basic forms of mental illness, neurosis and psychosis. But let us first emphasize that neurosis affects far more females than males, while psychosis affects far more males than females.

Both conditions, as I claim, arise from the failure of the two brains, of the two beings within us, to get along in harmony. In mental illness, the two are at odds with each other, in conflict with each other.

In neurosis, the cerebellar being—which, from now on, we will refer to by Jung's term, "the Self" (*not* by Freud's term, "the unconscious," because the Self is, of course, an alternative *consciousness*)—is, so to speak, punishing and subjugating the cerebral being—which, from now on, we will refer to as the Ego. There is a wide range of neurotic conditions—duodenal ulcers, anorexia, sleepwalking, multiple personality, and so forth.

But in psychosis and schizophrenia, the Ego attempts to split from, to shut out, and to deny the Self completely and totally. This results in true madness and insanity. Paradoxically, in the attempt to escape completely from the Self, in attempting to be totally and permanently in the objective world of waking consciousness, the Ego now actually loses that real, objective world! The world it now lives in is a world of its own—a *mad* world.

Our two basic personae, the Self and the Ego, are very different from each other—they are opposites in many ways.

We should point out here that nature very often works with, makes its progress by, pairs of opposites: thus we have male/female; plant/animal; the crossing of widely divergent species to produce new species; and so on. Probably all this goes back ultimately to the basic polarity of this universe, that is, the positive and negative electromagnetic poles present in every atom.

The Ego is one single personality. The Self is a collection of personalities—not one unit at all—thus we have many personae of dreams and the different forms we ourselves can assume in dreaming; we have many personalities that speak through us in trance and in hypnosis; we have the phenomenon of the condition of multiple personality; and so on.

What needs to be emphasized further here is that (a) religion is a form of "trance" and "neurosis," whereas (b) science and objectivity are forms of "psychosis" and "schizophrenia." There is no objection to either of these conditions or approaches, providing they remain within their own frames of reference and, most importantly, do not *deny* each other.

Religion is *not* objectively real. Religion is an aspect of our personality. It is a product of the cerebellar consciousness. God and the devil are products of our cerebellar consciousness.

You doubt that! Well, guess what? Mohammed, the founder of the Muslim religion, was spoken to *in trance* by the Angel Gabriel, who instructed him to set up Islam. Mohammed also saw visions of angels in trance.

As we have established, the Self has a wide range of different sub-personalities. And religion *also* has many different forms—Christianity, Islam, Judaism, Buddhism, and so on. But moreover, within each main religion there are *also* many sub-varieties. Thus in Christianity, we have Catholics, Protestants, Quakers, Mormons, Eastern Orthodoxes, Jehovah's Witnesses, and the like. And, of course, in *objective* terms, the whole religious situation is fundamentally and logically unacceptable. For example, if the Christians are correct and Christ was indeed the Son of God—then all members of other religions who reject that view will burn in hell. But if the other religions are correct in their rejection of this matter, then the Christians are simply nutters.

Sidetracking a little—we noted already that Christianity and Judaism have many features derived from the moon religion of the Neanderthals. One we have not mentioned in regard to Judaism is that it is recommended to Jewish married couples to make love on the Sabbath! A clear echo of orgiastic moon worship. And guess what?—the Muslim religious calendar is *directly* based on the phases of the moon! Thus the beginning of Ramadan, for example, is signaled by the new moon. (And, of course, many Arab flags display the crescent moon.) Also, the Muslim holy day is, like that of the Jews, Friday—and Friday, as we know, is Freija's day, the day of the Moon Goddess.

As already stated, there is no objection to religion/faith/belief on its own terms. On the contrary, this is the gateway to psychic healing, to self-healing, to genuine visions of future events, and so on. It is when religion attempts to impose itself on the objective world, or on the religious views of others—when it condones the actual killing of disbelievers, suicide bombing, and so on—it is then we are talking about *real* and *clinical* neurosis, without the quotation marks.

Similarly, when science denies the reality of psychic healing, or the ability of humans and animals to see the future, and so on—then we are talking of psychosis and schizophrenia, without the quotation marks.

But the positive scenario is when we accept the existence, the independence, the differing roles of both our personalities, of *both* the Self and the Ego. Then the gains are enormous.

We have already seen instances of acclaimed artists of various kinds who derive or have derived their inspiration *directly* from dreams and trance—that is, from the functioning of the Self. But the *fact* is that many scientists also state that they receive direct and detailed inspiration from this same source.

Niels Bohr, for example, who won the Nobel Prize for his work in physics, reports that he dreamed his model of the atom. August Kekulé von Stradonitz also attributed his interpretation of the structure of the benzene molecule to a dream. As did Otto Loewi in regard to his experiment on frog nerves, which again led to his receiving a Nobel Prize. Several other leading scientists have also attested to hitting on major discoveries while daydreaming or in reverie.

Returning to the notion of "two universes," the ability of psychic archaeologists to discover buried objects and cities *might* possibly be attributed to these objects emitting some sort of radiation—although for a receipt or a will hidden in a secret compartment to do that is hard to imagine. But we also have the matter of the ability to see the future—the ability to see, in detail, events that have not yet occurred in normal space-time. So these events clearly exist, somehow exist, *before* they have actually happened. The future, at least bits of it, is already there. And the (unknown) past, at least bits of it, is still there. Amazing, but true.

The *fact*, the *proven fact*, that aspects of the future in some sense exist before they have happened in our normal space-time, of course, totally rules out the notion that our normal space-time is the only dimension in existence—the only universe in existence.

So there exists *also*, there also *exists,* some kind of dimension, or universe, some frame of reference other than that of the normal space-time.

Sorry, scientists, but this is a *fact.* You must put your thinking caps on and try to sort that one out. But it may well be, of course, that the alternative universe is available to, accessible by, the Self. And that the religious view, say, of eternity does, after all, have validity.

What's to be done? On to our next chapter.

Chapter 12

The Madness of Science Equals the Madness of Religion

THIS CHAPTER, LIKE THE first, is a direct appeal to students (though equally to the media)—an appeal for *action*. Students worldwide must band together to create this revolution. For it is absolutely clear that our half-brained/single-brained scientists will never do it.

It is the undeniable case that 50 percent of our history is missing—but much more importantly still, that 50 percent of our psychology is missing. The many, many items we have cited do not appear anywhere in our textbooks, or as part of any university or college course.

Yet telepathy is a *fact,* sir/madam, it *is*. Psychic healing is a *fact*. The ability to produce wounds on the body simply by thinking about them is a *fact*. The ability to see the future is a *fact*. The ability to see the unknown past is a *fact*. Poltergeist phenomena are a *fact*. Paranormal fire is a *fact*. Spontaneous self-combustion is a *fact*.

And so on and so on.

What needs to happen, then, is that the cerebellum and its powers—that is, dream consciousness and the Self—must be raised to equal level with the cerebrum and waking consciousness (the Ego). These matters must become part, an *equal* part, of our university courses, our text-books, our training programs.

Not only must the material concerned be incorporated into the curricula of our universities, colleges, and schools—but it would also be advisable to have colleges and training centers concerned *specifically* with these matters—and which could concentrate on talented individuals in these areas and concerns, just as engineering colleges concentrate on those who are good at engineering, drama colleges concentrate on those who are gifted in acting, and so on.

What we must also do, of course, is to remove the management of religion from the hands of the existing priests, clerics, and the various religious faiths.

Our priests and religionists are wholly misguided in their view and interpretation of religion.

That is to say, the *details* of the various religions, are, of course, of no importance. In Judaism, for instance, a male baby has to be circumcised. No Jew may eat the flesh of pigs. Milk and meat may not be consumed in the same meal. But what does any of this *matter?* Answer—it doesn't.

Priests and religionists must be made to understand and accept that God and the devil and, of course, miracles—are *human behaviors.* They are aspects of the Self. They are the products of our cerebellum.

But *yes,* these powers do produce miracles. Yes, they *do* give access to another universe, one that lies outside the framework of normal space and time.

And *yes,* they might even give us immortality!

Who knows the limits of what the cerebellum and the Self might achieve, given the chance? As set out earlier, we already know for a *fact* that an individual riddled with disease, and on the brink of death, can be cured and resurrected in the space of a few hours. So might the Self and the cerebellum also be able to *halt* or *reverse* the aging process, effectively granting us immortality?

On the one hand, we have to free the Self (and its powers) from its current total exclusion by the scientific and academic communities. But equally, on the other hand, it must be freed from its current (and totally incorrect) dominance by religious groups—from those groups' very, very serious misunderstanding of the Self's nature and source.

There remains the question of our political polarities. That is probably an even harder matter to deal with. But certainly publicizing the source of our right-wing/left-wing duality would be a first step in resolving this conflict.

We should, in fact, disband our political parties completely. We need, want just one party—the party of common sense, of reasonableness, of open-mindedness.

To create a Neanderthal society—which is effectively what is happening in the world—is no better, no more acceptable a solution than was the creation of a Nazi state in Germany.

Steadily increasing Neanderthalism—socialism—in Britain has led to, and will continue to lead to, a significant rise in level of crime, in cheating and double-dealing (for example, in terms of abusing social services and benefits), one-parent families, the spread of sexually transmitted diseases and teenage pregnancies, the dumbing down of education (so that today record numbers of children are illiterate and innumerate), the "human rights" fiasco (whereby, for instance, known and dangerous terrorists cannot be named, whereby so-called asylum seekers are effectively given a lifetime of benefits and free housing), and so on and so on.

These criticisms are no kind of plea for a return to right-wing "values"; let us point out, for instance, that Jews, representing something like 0.1 percent of the world's population, nevertheless win 25 percent of the Nobel Prizes. They also have the highest average IQ of any group, at 115. And it was *these* people that the stupid Nazis set out to destroy!

Nor must we fail to underline the inadequacy of our scientific and academic establishments. We have repeatedly demonstrated their inadequacy throughout this book. But let's have one more detailed example.

The scientific establishment maintains, and has always maintained, that Cro-Magnons emerged from *Africa* some 60,000 years ago. (But today, one or two anthropologists are suggesting that the Cro-Magnons might have evolved in Asia.)

So, according to orthodox science, in the space of 60,000 years:

1. black skin becomes white skin
2. brown eyes become blue eyes
3. frizzy black hair becomes straight blond hair (with a different cross-section)
4. dense bones become light bones
5. recessive chin becomes a jutting chin
6. prognathous mouth becomes a flattened mouth
7. full lips become thin lips
8. extended occiput (the rear of the head) becomes a flattened occiput
9. large cerebellum becomes a smaller cerebellum
10. significant increase in male body and facial hair and a significant increase in male-pattern baldness
11. significant drop in sex drive (blacks in America and Britain make love on average twelve times a week, whites an average of twice a week)
12. significant rise in the age at which boys and girls reach puberty
13. significant increase in intelligence

So all these *dramatic* changes occurred in the space of 60,000 years, did they, sir/madam? (And in response to what *precise* environmental pressures? Any suggestions, sir/madam?)

But the above list is only part of the story, only part of the evidence involved.

We have, for instance, the blushing of females to indicate sexual arousal—not just the face turns red, incidentally, but the upper chest also. Then we have the reddening of the male face (and again the upper chest) to indicate anger. Such ethnological signals long predate the emergence of speech—they are hundreds of thousands, if not millions of years old. *They could only have evolved, in any case, in a creature with white skin.*

Then again we have the instinctive urge of Europeans (that is, Cro-Magnons) to sunbathe. Sunlight is one of the very few sources of vitamin D—and without vitamin D children develop rickets, as do children from places like India living today in towns in northern Europe. So Cro-Magnons must have evolved in conditions of poor sunlight, toward the north of Asia/Europe, and hence evolved the instinctive urge to sunbathe.

(*One* of the reasons, of course, why Cro-Magnons were sun-worshippers!)

(We should mention here my view that Neanderthals had certainly discovered that fish liver is another source of vitamin D. And fish, of course, live in water, the domain of the Moon Goddess. This is the reason for the role of the fish in the Christian religion—another of the bits of the ancient moon religion that we have not discussed, although we have mentioned the Fisher King.)

So, in short, those scientist and academics who have maintained (and still maintain) that Cro-Magnons came out of Africa 60,000 years ago should be sacked. That's effectively all of them!

Am I giving you enough ammunition for your revolution, students? I hope so.

Conclusion
And Finally . . .

THE SCIENTIFIC AND ACADEMIC establishments have from day one refused to comment on my claims and views—much less to take them on board in any way. But, as already stated more than once, with passing time more and more of my, as it were, "wild and unfounded" claims have been proven.

In complete contrast to the establishment position, however, my books and their contents have from day one received widespread and unequivocal acclaim from book reviewers. Some samples of these reviews follow in the last appendix.

Some final comments in conclusion.

Osama Bin Laden is left-handed.

Returning to the matter of pedophilia—as stated earlier, the fact that the bonobo chimpanzees routinely practice this very strongly suggests that this was also a perfectly normal behavior for Neanderthals. Pedophilia was, then, one of the cards in the original Neanderthal pack—and we are each of us dealt a hand from the two shuffled Neanderthal and Cro-Magnon packs.

What we now know, thanks to the Internet and its use, is that there are considerably more—far more—pedophiles in the general population than was previously thought. What is also very significant is that a very large majority of pedophiles are in every other respect perfectly normal—they are happily married with children of their own, can be successful teachers, doctors, clergy, business men and women, whatever. The latest case mentioned in the media is that of a life-long vicar who had a collection of 100,000 pictures showing children being sexually "abused." (We put the word *abused* in quotation marks because the condemnation is a Cro-Magnon point of view.) Nor have the large majority of pedophiles themselves been ill-treated, victimized, or sexually "abused" themselves in any way during childhood.

My own view, of course, is that if large numbers of pedophiles were examined, they would show a higher incidence of left-handedness (just as do lesbians and homosexuals), a greater incidence of the big toe being shorter than the second toe, a greater proportion of sleep being spent in dreaming, shorter height, a higher incidence of the simian line—and so on for all the other Neanderthal characteristics we have listed earlier.

Quite what the solution is to our possessing two sets of opposing instincts is not easy to see. Some of us will always favor a Cro-Magnon point of view, and others a Neanderthal view.

The answer is certainly not to enforce Cro-Magnon standards, as the Nazis set out to do. But neither is the solution to (further) encourage the current Neanderthalization of our society—being soft on crime, lowering or totally abandoning educational standards, tolerating religious extremism, allowing rights without duties, and so on.

One of the very significant items in the current trend of Neanderthalization is the abandonment of the vision that intelligence, skills, ability, and indeed *all* behaviors and traits are at least 90 percent genetically determined. They have (in objective fact, as opposed to wishful thinking and subjective conviction) very little to do with opportunity, education, training, domestic background, upbringing, or whatever. Environmental factors are of very little importance (except in *very* extreme situations).

And if it is not/were not the case that genetic factors are by far the overriding and dominant decider, then why and how is it, Mr. Neanderthal, that animal breeders can augment (or remove) the qualities, both physical and mental, that they require in a species or variety by selective breeding? This is what animal breeding is *all* about, isn't it?

And why don't the environmentally persuaded, those who believe it is all about opportunity and encouragement, take groups of children (infants), chosen at random, and turn these individuals into—say— accomplished composers; gifted artists; brilliant actors; outstanding singers; or any other kind of superior performer or genius?

The answer is, they don't because they *can't*. Because these various matters are all about genetic endowment, not opportunity or training. (And the genetically endowed will always, where necessary, create their own opportunities.)

I don't think I've commented specifically on zombies and vampires. Both of these are memories of Neanderthals.

When during a battle or fight a Neanderthal went into a trance state, normal wounding had little or no effect in stopping him. He was the "walking," the "fighting" dead. Only a really serious wound could stop him. And so that's why, in legend, to kill a vampire, you had to drive a stake through its heart.

The vampire, of course, drank blood. And there is no doubt at all that Neanderthals drank the blood and ate the flesh of sacrificial victims in religious ceremonies. And that is why, as already stated, Catholics drink the blood and eat the flesh of Christ during Mass. And why, again as we already know, Australian Aborigines eat the foreskin of the circumcised boy at his manhood ceremony.

The trance states of Neanderthals were stranger than our own because of Neanderthal's larger and more powerful cerebellum.

As cannot be stressed too often, the cerebellum—the back brain totally excluded by our psychologists—is responsible for trance states, for dreams, for telepathy, for psychic healing, for spontaneous wounds, for poltergeist phenomena, and *all* other such matters.

It is also the source of and the impetus for religious belief.

And whereas we have but one consciousness in regard to the

cerebrum, the front brain—our normal waking consciousness—the consciousness of the cerebellum is multifaceted. It is a multiconsciousness, so to speak. Thus and thence, we have the many figures produced during the neurotic illness of multiple personality (when the cerebellar consciousness invades and takes over cerebral consciousness), and, of course, the myriad figures (the alleged "departed spirits") produced by psychic mediums during trance. And, of course, once again, the many varieties of religion.

We have one science. But many religions.

So this is the scenario you must bring to center stage, students. All this is the material and ammunition for your revolution and rebellion.

Lastly, a coincidental (?) item.

The number thirteen figures centrally in my work because it is the most important number of the moon religion. And it just so happens that I was born on June 13. And the day, it just so happens, was a Monday. And Monday is, of course, Moon Day.

So I was born on Moon Day the 13th. Duality is, of course, also central to my work. And as it again just so happens, the zodiac sign for June is Gemini—the twins. Well, well, well . . .

Appendix 1

The Sphinx

THE ITEMS IN THIS appendix are further support for the evidence and statements in parts 1 and 2.

First Neanderthal.

The recent discoveries of early human remains in both Portugal and Israel are, as already stated, proof that Neanderthals and Cro-Magnons did interbreed:

> The bones (back of head, lower jaw, shoulder blades) display features that were characteristic of our evolutionary cousins, the Neanderthals.
>
> PROFESSOR ERIK TRINKAUS

> We've known for some time that the earliest modern humans in Europe are a funny looking bunch. They are a distinctive looking lot, very heavily built, especially in the skulls.
>
> PROFESSOR CLIVE GAMBLE

The Lagar Velho boy (from Portugal) who died some 25,000 years ago has, in particular, been defined as a hybrid with a mixture of modern and Neanderthal features:

A 24,500 year old skeleton found in a hillside in Portugal shows the unmistakeable characteristics of both Homo Sapiens and Neanderthal man, two species that were known to co-exist in Europe but assumed never to have interbred. Scientists now say that the skeleton of a boy of four could be the true ancestor of all modern humans.

DAILY EXPRESS, APRIL 1999

But now these already indisputable finds have, in any case, been confirmed by recent DNA studies:

I have started reading and researching at full speed and have traced the scientists who are responsible for recent claims of Cro-Magnon/Neanderthal interbreeding. These scientists claim to have found "the most robust genetic evidence to date confirming that humans and Neanderthals interbred when they co-existed together thousands of years ago."

HEIDI ALLEMEERSCH,
SCIENCE JOURNALIST, 2006

So interbreeding between Neanderthal and Cro-Magnon is now effectively a fact *also* in DNA, an establishment-accepted fact—although some scientists continue not to accept this evidence of interbreeding. But, of course, as cannot be emphasized enough, we already had/have the required proof in the bone-mixture data.

The DNA scientists concerned say that they consider the input of Neanderthal genes into our earlier gene pool was fairly small—a situation I am quite happy to accept. The crucial point is—as already stated in part 1—that the originally small input of Neanderthal genes *has steadily increased over the intervening tens of thousands of years.* The reason for this is that Neanderthals were far more sexually active and fertile—as are/were the individuals who received the input of the Neanderthal genes.

So we are *more* Neanderthal today than we ever were. And, of course, as already emphasized in part 1, several well-known writers apart from myself have pointed out that "you can observe Neanderthal at any public gathering." (All you need to confirm this, scientists, is that you have a pair of eyes in your head—but I appreciate that most of you don't have them.)

One of the many outcomes of this situation, as we cannot stress too often, is the emergence and ever-growing dominance of the left-wing political movement, of left-wing thinking. Communism and socialism are, according to me, the Neanderthals' view of the world and the universe.

Among the many other matters for which orthodox science has no explanation—it has none, of course, for the above, that is, why should a single species produce two totally opposed political viewpoints—is the emergence of art in the human scenario.

Fully developed art—that is, perfect modern art—leaps into sudden existence some 30,000 years ago, out of nowhere. In Aurignac in the southwest of France, we have more than 300 cave paintings of bears, mammoths, rhinos, and so on, in many different colors, with many of the animals actually leaping and running.

These are perfectly modern paintings, and, as noted, they appear from nowhere, overnight. We have no evidence whatsoever, anywhere, of any gradual learning, of any gradual evolution, and "coincidentally," of course, at the same time as and also in the area where Cro-Magnons and Neanderthals interbred. (What a coincidence!)

This is, of course, an excellent example of "hybrid vigor"—the fact that new hybrid species produced by the crossing of two widely divergent species show totally new behaviors, possessed by neither parental strain.

(Well, conventional scientists and anthropologists, how do *you* account for the sudden explosion of fully developed art? You don't. You can't.)

And then, of course, at precisely this same time, we have also a sudden and dramatic explosion in new, complex tools. This is a well-documented and accepted *fact*. Nobody disputes it. But nobody has any explanation for it.

The indisputable and undisputed case is that neither Cro-Magnon nor Neanderthal tools had shown any change for thousands of years. Both species had been stuck in a complete rut.

There now follows an article written by David Percy, titled "The Face of the Sphinx."

The evidence continues to mount that the Great Sphinx, the temple buildings associated with it, and the Giza Pyramids are considerably older than Egyptian civilization.

John Anthony West (in his book *Serpent in the Sky*), using rainwater erosion as his criterion and now backed in his judgment by geologist Dr. Robert Schoch, gives the Sphinx a minimum age of 9,000 years BP, but is willing to go much further. Bauval and Gilbert, in their 1994 book *The Orion Mystery* and using star alignments as their criteria, favor 10,450 BC as the most likely date for the inception of the pyramids.

I have my own grounds for considering that these various structures long predate the Egyptian civilization, and these are set out in detail in the book I coauthored with David Myers, *Two-Thirds: A History of Our Galaxy*, first published in 1993. We will come to some of those reasons later.

However, as it happened, in 1994 I saw the BBC *TimeWatch* TV documentary *Age of the Sphinx* on John Anthony West's theories in company with the author Stan Gooch. After the program I put the question to Stan: What did he consider that, in particular, the face of the Sphinx represents? I had not discussed this matter with him on any previous occasion, nor was it a point he had himself previously considered.

It must be mentioned by way of background that Stan, most notably in his latest book *Cities of Dreams*, has long argued that our early ancestors, the Neanderthals, far from being more or less speechless brutes, as they are conventionally portrayed, had evolved a highly developed religious civilization. Why then, one asks, has no trace of this alleged civilization survived? Gooch's answer, in short, is that it has, both in legend and in structures such as that of the Cretan maze—where, as is well known, Theseus is said to have slain the Minotaur (that is, the Neanderthals themselves).

At any rate, Stan's answer to my question, after he had studied a number of photographs and drawings of the Sphinx, was that he considered the head of the Sphinx to be a deliberate and quite "unnatural" combination of Neanderthal characteristics (nose, mouth, and jaw) with characteristics of the Neanderthal's later successor, the Cro-Magnon (eyes, brows, crown, and ears).

As it happens, orthodoxy does not dispute the possibility that Neanderthals and Cro-Magnons met and mingled genetically in the Middle East some 35,000 years ago. This view is based on several actual skeletons with dramatically mixed characteristics found on Mount Carmel (the Tabūn and Skūhl finds). Israel, incidentally, is also the only country in the world where pure Neanderthal and Cro-Magnon remains have been found side by side.

The Tabūn bones were Neanderthal, the Skūhl bones were Cro-Magnon (now termed early modern *Homo sapiens*). More Neanderthals were found in the caves of Kebara on Mount Carmel and near the Sea of Galilee at Amud. Meanwhile, investigators also discovered a larger find of Cro-Magnons buried at the Jebel Qafzeh cave near Nazareth, also in Galilee. However, among the Tabūn and Skūhl finds, researchers also found some examples of hybridization, as has been found in skulls found at Mladec in the Czech Republic. Further, six bones found in 1952 in the Romanian cave of Pestera Muierii have recently been reevaluated by Erik Trinkaus (now of Washington University in St. Louis).

Trinkaus and his colleagues dated these bones to 30,000 BP, but, controversially for some, found them to have Neanderthal characteristics as well as those of Cro-Magnon. There is also the Portuguese find: In 1998, the skeleton of a male child was unearthed at the Abrigo do Lagar Velho rock shelter in Portugal. The Lagar Velho boy, who died about 25,000 years ago, has been described as a "hybrid," with a mixture of modern and Neanderthal features.

Stan himself is now wholly convinced that the Sphinx is a monument to this human hybridization—which he personally considers gave birth to many of the vigorous abilities of ourselves, modern humans. Both animal and plant breeders do, of course, habitually cross widely divergent species in order to produce dramatically new strains, hence the term *hybrid vigor.* On this view of a monument to human hybridization, and in Stan's particular opinion, the Sphinx could be of very considerable antiquity, as much, in principle, as 35,000 years old.

What Stan did not know of at this point was the view that Myers and myself have proposed in *Two-Thirds* (published 1993). This book, although written in the form of an epic novel telling the story of human evolution, is based on data we have generated using a form of "far memory." We ourselves consider it to be essentially factual. At any rate, in our book the order given to the builder of the Sphinx (long prior to Egyptian civilization, incidentally) is this:

Modify the face of the statue (the Sphinx) to resemble both the face of the transitional self-aware being resulting from the *first part* of the genetic agent (Neanderthal) and the face of the being resulting from the *second part* of the genetic agent (Cro-Magnon).

PART 2, CHAPTER 10,

TWO-THIRDS: A HISTORY OF OUR GALAXY

After he had recovered from his astonishment on being shown this text, Stan and I then began the attempt to re-create the head of the Great Sphinx by combining a drawing of an actual Neanderthal skull with a drawing of an actual Cro-Magnon skull.

Figures A.1a and A.1b show the complete skulls of actual Neanderthal and Cro-Magnon, respectively. A.1c shows the result of combining the lower section of the former (unchanged) and the upper section of the latter (unchanged) plus the superimposition of this new combined skull on the head of the Sphinx. The reader will form his or her own judgment as to the goodness of this fit. We consider it excellent.

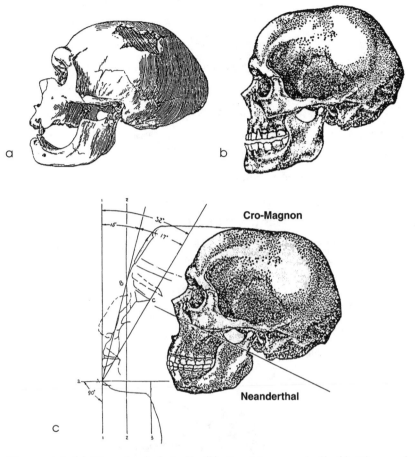

Figure A.1 (a) Neanderthal skull; (b) Cro-Magnon skull; (c) The result of combining the lower section of the Neanderthal skull and the upper section of the Cro-Magnon skull and superimposing this new combined skull on the head of the Sphinx. (Based on Sphinx profile drawn by Frank Domingo.)

There are further factors. Stan Gooch has long held totally heretical views on the anatomy and physiology of the Neanderthals (such as considering them to be left-handed), which the scientific community has refused to countenance. Nevertheless, with passing time, more and more of Stan's views are being confirmed. One of these concerns the Neanderthal's nose. Stan has always maintained that Jews have a larger admixture of Neanderthal genes, certainly than any European group—

and that anti-Semitism is in fact anti-Neanderthalism. Then in 1988, Robert Franciscus and Erik Trinkaus, then of the University of New Mexico, published in the *American Journal of Physical Anthropology* their finding that Neanderthals had far larger noses than modern humans, an average 34 millimeters broad compared with an average 25 millimeters broad, which also projected at least as far out as the most projecting modern nose, and probably further. One of the most persistent views of the anti-Semite is, of course, that Jews have big noses.

Figure A.2 shows a reconstruction of a Neanderthal with a large nose added. By no coincidence whatsoever, this reconstruction looks both Jewish and American Indian. Stan has long maintained that the Jews are the people with the strongest dose of Neanderthal genes.

The face of the Great Sphinx as we see it today is damaged (see figure A.3). It has been claimed that it was used at some point in the past as a target by the military, when the then-existing nose was shot off. Napoleon's soldiers were among those suspected of this crime. However, the idea that Napoleon's men actually had anything to do with the damage to the nose of the Sphinx has been withdrawn by archaeologists. The

Figure A.2. Reconstruction of Neanderthal with large nose.

Figure A.3. The Great Sphinx today, with damaged nose. (Photo by Caroline Davies.)

most popular current theory is that the Turkish army destroyed the nose of the Sphinx during target practice.

But this claim is not supported by any credible primary data. There is no evidence that the military did any such thing as "shoot off" the nose. The question is, why would they demolish only the nose, so precisely as to not damage the other parts of the statue? If an army had so little respect for the structure, surely they wouldn't stop at the nose. It is unlikely that it was the handiwork of some phantom Napoleonic armory or even Turkish sharpshooters.

Some have argued that the Sphinx has a Negroid lower face. (A portrait of the Pharaoh Chephren it is definitely not!) But Stan Gooch and myself say that this is no typical Negroid mouth and chin—the lips are wrong, for example: they are full but not everted. Then the further suggestion by those who favor this Negroid hypothesis is that the Sphinx had the bridgeless Negroid nose. Yet that would hardly have formed an adequate foundation for suggesting that it was an inviting target for soldiers' cannon, would it?

We are convinced that the original Sphinx had the full Neanderthal/ Jewish nose, and figure A.1c (page 139) incorporates an impression of the Sphinx nose profile as we believe it originally was.

So, have we solved a little more of the riddle of the Sphinx—while opening the door to further wonders? I feel our case to be very strong. We have, after all, used actual Neanderthal and Cro-Magnon skulls, and our joining of these has produced a very good approximation of the head; and, of course, the bones found in the caves of Skühl and Tabün on Mount Carmel and elsewhere actually do exist.

I believe that we have here provided solid further general support for the view that the Great Sphinx and the other Giza structures are, in fact, far, far older than orthodoxy will currently accept.

I have not mentioned so far in the present book my view that the Neanderthal had a very large projecting nose. One of my reasons for this view is that I consider present-day Jews to have the largest admixture of Neanderthal genes of any current human group. The big Jewish nose is, of course, a feature often commented on and derided.

The large Jewish nose of the Neanderthal is now accepted by orthodoxy. The *Daily Telegraph* (June 6, 1988) published an article concerning a then-current article in the *American Journal of Physical Anthropology:*

> The secret of Neanderthals' big nose has been found, according to American scientists who claim that it was designed to cope with reasonably cold and dry environments. Neanderthal had a nose about 34 millimetres wide, compared with today's 23–28 millimetres. "It was at least as or more projecting than the most projecting modern nose," said Mr. Robert Franciscus, who has studied Neanderthal fossils with Dr. Erik Trinkaus of the University of New Mexico.

So my own view is that the Egyptian Sphinx is, in fact, a monument to the miracle of human hybridization. We have—there is—of course, no other available reason for the existence of the Sphinx. But surely one is needed.

There follows now the first part of the interview already mentioned in part 2.

Q.1. You wrote your first creative book, *Total Man*—your first non-textbook—when you were in your late thirties. What made you start creative writing so late in life?

A.1. Good question—though just for the record, I had already written a novel, which didn't get published, but did get me a job as script-reader for Paramount Pictures. But yes—you are asking, in effect, whether I had intended to become a writer, and the answer to that is no. I had never had any idea what I wanted to do with my life—except that from day one, I had a very strong drive to collect information, to learn about everything. As a youngster, for instance, I set myself the task of reading every single book in the local public library—and pretty much managed it. It was no problem at all for me to read two or three books in a single day.

Q. 2. So what caused you to write *Total Man*?

A. 2. Well, I knew a scout from Penguin Books (Eddie Luttwak—who went on to write a couple of books of his own, but ended up as Professor of Warfare—or some such title—and became a close advisor to the government on armaments) who was aware that I had written a novel and wanted to write more such—but he asked me whether I had any ideas for nonfiction books. At once I said yes, I could write a book on the real nature of humankind. So I thereupon wrote a draft outline and gave it to Eddie the next day. A couple of days later Penguin wrote commissioning the book, and giving me an advance of £500, which in those days was a considerable sum, a few thousand at today's prices.

More to the point, though, is that I then sat down and wrote the book straight out from start to finish. In the morning, I would produce some 2,000 to 3,000 words, in the afternoon I would type out the previous day's 3,000. I did bits of research too—checking on figures and quotes. But the book was finished in three months, some 200,000 words in all (550 pages), a long book by any standards.

So the whole book was really ready there in my mind, all worked out and waiting, it just needed the tap turned on. Yet I had given it no conscious thought, beyond the central idea itself (the duality of our being). How can this situation be? You will find no mention whatever of this incredible creative facility of the human mind in modern psychology textbooks, much less any kind of explanation. Mozart's music poured out in the same way, and so is the case with many other individuals in the various creative fields.

Q.3. This is a mental function that is possessed only by an outstanding, highly intelligent few, is it?

A.3. No, not at all. I've referred to gifted individuals (if I'm allowed to be included in that category myself!). But take, for instance, Jane Roberts, who writes the numerous *Seth* books. She writes these books—so she believes—by taking dictation from her spirit guide. Now, I don't myself rate these books, nor do I consider them "true" in any factual sense. That's not the point. The point is that these books—and all the other books written by automatic writing, all the artworks produced by automatic drawing, all the music produced by automatic composing—are delivered already *complete*. Let's not forget, of course, Dr. Anita Mühl's mental patients—some of whom wrote their stories out *backward*, and one who could write two different texts simultaneously with her two hands, while at the same time reading aloud from a newspaper!

The latest astonishing example of automatic writing is David Myers's *Two-Thirds: A History of Our Galaxy*. This book was, he believes, dictated to him by a source known as "Tom," spokesman for the Council of Nine—a group of wise, universal nonphysical beings. The entire text "came" to Myers, literally word by word. The book contains, among other matters, a good deal of mathematics and some remarkable statements about human evolution. There is, in fact, a lot of science in the work, very unusual in this type of production. I know David Myers personally, and have had long chats with "Tom" while David is in trance. But when I say trance, David is perfectly capable, meanwhile, of driving a car along a busy motorway—at the same time communicating as "Tom"!

Q.4. Can I pull you up there—before you get completely carried away—and come back to the matter of your own development? Can you tell us something more about your early years?

A.4. Yes, of course. Well, as I said, I was a kind of vacuum cleaner sucking up knowledge, but with no idea why, really. In the course of my "controlled drifting," as I used to describe my lack of a definable goal to my puzzled contemporaries, I acquired a degree in modern languages, then a degree in psychology. I worked mainly as a teacher (which included a spell teaching severely maladjusted children) and a research psychologist—though my first job after leaving college was in the scrap metal business. Maybe there's some significance in that! But also in my spare time, I pursued at the practical level, for instance, organic gardening and folk dancing, and, in fact, all kinds of alternative activities. I had also come across the ideas of spiritualism, notably through Conan Doyle's *Land of Mist,* and so, having got to know one or two practicing spiritualists, I went to my first séance. There a crucial event happened—I went into trance. As I describe it, it seemed to me that the room was full of rushing, deafening water—a great tidal wave picked me up and hurled me forward (therefore from behind, please note), and I fell unconscious. Some huge barrier had been breached. While I was unconscious several entities spoke through me. I had become a medium—just like that. Thereafter I joined a mediumistic development group—and quickly produced all the various mediumistic abilities, such as automatic writing and causing objects in the room to move. All this was before I took my psychology degree. And incidentally, while reading for my psychology degree, I underwent a full Jungian psychoanalysis. So the "alternative universe" that modern academics and scientists so pointedly ignore was fully real and actual to me.

Q.5. Well, we can begin to understand your fascination with the dual nature of humankind, because you have had so much experience of both sides. I mean, apart from your, in fact, two textbooks on child development, you have published many scientific papers in the various learned journals and magazines. For you, the unconscious is every bit as real and meaningful as the conscious.

A.5. Yes—except that I don't at all like "conscious" and "unconscious." To describe the duality of the human personality, I prefer the terms Ego and Self (conscious and unconscious, respectively). These are, if you like, two adjacent and largely independent, though continuously interacting, kingdoms—equal, though certainly opposite in their endowments and functions. The Ego is heavily concerned in the normal activities of daily waking life—including important items like mathematics and science, all forms of *objectivity*. The Self is paramount in matters such as dreaming, hypnosis, trance mediumship, psychic healing—all so-called paranormal activities, in fact—and, importantly, the current flood of so-termed UFO experiences, abductions and whatever.

Here now is an article I wrote for *The Ley Hunter.*

In this all too brief article, I shall compare the views of our origins put forward, in basically four books with those I have proposed, in my own writings, notably in my most recent book *Cities of Dreams*. The four other books in question are *The Sirius Mystery* by Robert Temple, *Fingerprints of the Gods* by Graham Hancock, *From Atlantis to the Sphinx* by Colin Wilson, and *The Sirius Connection* by Murry Hope.

The Sirius Mystery and *The Sirius Connection* are among the books which claim that civilization was seeded in peoples of our planet by visitors from outer space. *Fingerprints of the Gods* and *From Atlantis to the Sphinx* are among those that argue for an early "lost" human civilization some 10,000 or so years ago, which, following its destruction, nevertheless managed to seed its advanced knowledge and culture around our globe. For convenience, I shall refer to this alleged civilization by the terms *Atlantis* and *Atlantean*.

Let me say at the outset that these four books are quite staggering collections of precise information and scholarly research, with an accompanying wealth of fascinating anecdote and conjecture. They cannot be faulted on these scores nor on the sincerity and dedication of the authors concerned. Where I shall be severely faulting these writers, however, is (1) on the interpretations they put on this otherwise genuine material; (2) still more strongly on the mass of additional historical information that they and all others collectively ignore; and (3) on the absence of what, for shorthand purposes, I will call common sense.

Common sense? Well, for example, both Robert Temple and Murry Hope consider that the alien visitors came from a planet orbiting the star Sirius. Now, it just so happens that Sirius is the brightest star in the sky. What then are the chances of these visitors having come from that particular (or any particular) star? They are 100,000,000,000 to 1 against. One hundred thousand million to one. That statement does not, of course, in any way prove that the alleged visitors did not come from Sirius. But there is more. It just so happens that the first dawn rising of Sirius in Egyptian times marked the beginning of the "dog days"—the searing, parched days of summer (charged also, as we now know, with positive ions, leading to depression and other psychological conditions). Moreover, the star in this position glowed red. So the inference was that the "heat" of Sirius produced the subsequent burning. And it *just so happens* that the visitors from space came from that particular star, so notable in these and other important ways?

Of course, Temple and Hope make much of the fact that the ancients knew that Sirius is a binary star system—in this case, a blazing star orbited by a dead dwarf star. This fact was not discovered by science till the nineteenth century. However, Sirius periodically twinkles. Might not people who well understood that the moon orbits the earth, and the earth the sun (and such people *there certainly were*), hypothesize that the twinkling effect arose from the occasional intervention between viewer and viewed of an orbiting body? Yes, I think so. (There are many other points we could also make. Why did not the visitors tell the Egyptians of the importance of the human brain? When the Egyptians mummified a corpse, they threw the brain away—while preserving the heart, liver, and so on in special vessels.)

Theories of lost Atlantean civilizations suffer from similar common-sense deficiencies. One does not at all dispute that the Piri Reis maps and their earlier counterparts correctly show the outlines of the continent of Antarctica and its mountain ranges and former rivers—which are currently buried under one mile of solid ice and have been so throughout historical time. Therefore, someone did map the continent—what?—some 10,000 years ago when it was ice free. Hancock considers that Antarctica was the actual homeland of the Atlanteans. But in that case, then, *why do the maps not show any towns* or any place names?

Still others, however, say that although the Atlanteans mapped Antarctica, they did not live there. Their (wherever) homeland was swallowed up, suddenly, in some other way. (Shame, though, that there aren't any maps of *that* one to be found.)

Nevertheless, all Atlantean theorists say that the Atlanteans were highly civilized and great seafarers. So then we have two possible scenarios. (1) The Atlanteans were explorers and seafarers who, either simply as explorers or perhaps even as traders, visited many parts of the world. (2) Although they were great seafarers, they did not make any significant contact with other peoples until the point when their world was overwhelmed by flood or ice. Then they took to their boats and went to South America, the Middle East, and wherever, taking their skills with them.

Whether we take scenario (1) or (2) or both, then surely we *must* find identical/similar artifacts of Atlantean design (weapons—pots—instruments—coins?), even if only in very small quantities scattered throughout the world—and certainly in both Egypt and South America. But there is not one single identical artifact or manufactured object of any kind that is found in both these locations. How could the Atlanteans have not left their physical fingerprints everywhere? (Similarly, of course, we do not have one single solitary artifact of any kind anywhere in the world of extraterrestrial origin.)

Ah, but what of the pyramids? They are found in both Egypt and South America, and elsewhere. Yes, indeed—but the pyramid is a concept. And certainly there are many, many concepts we find everywhere in the world. We shall come to those.

In connection with concepts, however, a major problem—which is fully confronted, though not solved, by, for instance, Hancock and Hope (and more notably before them by Giorgio de Santillana, professor of the history of science at the Massachusetts Institute of Technology)—is why the universal "ancient wisdom" is always expressed in the form of stories, myths, and legends. Astronomical fact, calculations, structure are never expressed as we today express them—as a scientific formula, a table of periodicity, a mathematical equation. Instead, the numbers (including the squares, the integers, whatever) are put into a narrative. So this god takes these many dragon's teeth and hides them in a particular constellation, where they multiply and are recovered in these many quantities by the god's sister a thousand years later—and so on and so on.

The only explanation offered will not do—these are the words of Murry Hope. The solution to "the problems faced by an advanced race when trying to convey their great fund of knowledge to an unlettered people deeply enmeshed in the shrouds of superstition, the rational aspects of their brains lacking the appropriate stimulation" is to "personalize" the facts by means of stories. Well, that is complete rubbish. If we could pluck an intelligent youngster from 50,000 years back into the present, he or she would have no problem in learning math, chemistry, physics. Just as, by way of good example, the chimpanzee today has itself not evolved language. But we can readily *teach* a chimpanzee (sign) language. The chimp then uses the language meaningfully in new situations just as we do (for example, by referring to its keeper as an "arsehole" when he fails to produce a requested treat!) and also teaches the language to other chimps.

The answer—as I will briefly show—to the problem of why ancient scientific wisdom is couched exclusively in parables and stories is, *because it always was*. That was the form in which it was originally conceived. In that form it is strange only to us. To its originators this was the proper, correct, and normal way of expressing and encoding knowledge for handing it on to other individuals and the next generation.

One example now of the kind of material found worldwide which, both to myself and to all the authors concerned, is proof that long ago one central source must have been responsible for it (aliens in the case of outer spacers, Atlantis in the case of Atlanteans). However, I must stress that this is *my* example, not one of theirs—the Australian Aborigines are quite beneath their notice!

In ancient Greece, Orion the hunter amorously pursues six sisters and their mother through a wood. Zeus, overcome with compassion, changes both parties into stars—Orion pursuing the seven stars of the Pleiades. Among the Australian Aborigines, Wurrunna the hunter amorously pursues seven maidens. But seven trees grow magically tall and pluck the maidens into the sky to become the Pleiades. Among the Wyoming Indians of America, seven girls are hunted by a bear. They climb onto a rock, which suddenly grows high, pushing the girls into the sky to become the Pleiades.

As I have said, among the real problems for, and the real failures of, both outer-spacers and Atlanteans is that they totally ignore a mass of worldwide material (such as the foregoing), which is probably greater in bulk than anything they do use. There follows now what, in any case, is only a sample list of headings for the material concerned—each heading capable of expansion into a very long chapter.

1. The Pleiades. The only constellation *named and worshipped by every single culture and tribe on earth past and present.* This is a very tiny cluster of fourth-magnitude stars, very hard to spot at all.

2. The Australian Aborigines—more on this shortly.

3. The snake/serpent—which is also the dragon (that is, all dragons are stylized snakes). Probably the most ancient and central image humankind has (brought about Adam and Eve's downfall, as we know), along with:

4. The spider—more on this shortly.

5. The number seven (which *is* mentioned by Robert Temple). This one would need an entire book—it permeates everything. So, for example, we have seven units of time: seconds, minutes, hours, days, weeks, months, years.

6. The number thirteen—ditto as with seven, but this one has been heavily censored in historic time. Nevertheless, the God of Judaism has thirteen mystical aspects. The Greek pantheon originally had thirteen gods. The Scandinavian Valhalla originally had thirteen seats for gods. The number thirteen dominates South American calendars. It is the chief number of the Most Noble Order of the Garter. And the pyramid is the only 3-D object having a total of thirteen edges and surfaces (including the base).

7. Thirteen-zodiac. Preceded all twelve-zodiacs, of which the authors we are discussing make so much. Incidentally, King Arthur and his twelve knights of the *Round* Table are a disguised thirteen-zodiac. The spider is the thirteenth (censored) sign of the zodiac.

8. Thirteen-coven. All "founding" groups number thirteen: (in Australia) Baiani and his twelve followers; Christ and the twelve disciples; Roland and the twelve peers of France; Jacob and his twelve sons; Odysseus and his twelve companions; Hrolf and his twelve berserks; Romulus and the twelve shepherds; Robin Hood and his twelve men; the judge and twelve jurors; and so on.

9. Moon. A whole book is required on this one also. In all ancient cultures, the moon was worshipped as the snake and the spider (the main reason is given below). Most elements of so-called sun worship can be shown on examination to be moon elements. For example, the Aztec Great Temple of the Sun has 4 flights of 91 steps; $4 \times 91 = 364$ days, that is, the moon year of 13×28 days.

10. Cross (mentioned by Hancock, but not discussed). Ancient symbol for the moon, found in all cultures worldwide.

11. "Cretan" labyrinth. Found everywhere, always same basic model.

12. Left and left-handedness. Hated, feared, and despised in all cultures worldwide (yet many outstanding achievers are left-handed) and always associated with the feminine (though in all ethnic groups today, there are fewer left-handed women than men).

13. Menstruation. The seclusion, punishment, and almost deranged fear of the menstruating woman in all cultures worldwide.

Now, in this all-too-short article, we make a major leap. The following item appeared in the London *Times* on September 3, 1996, headed: "Cave Buries Neanderthal Man's Brutish Image":

Neanderthal man was a civilised creature according to intriguing evidence uncovered by a team of Spanish archaeologists. The key to their thesis lies in 15 furnaces, recently unearthed, dating back 53,000 years. Some were used for cooking, others as hearths to generate heat. Many served as rudimentary blast furnaces to make tools . . . an astonishing variety of tools . . . proof that Neanderthal possessed a skill level far more advanced than he has so far been given credit for.

There had, of course, been earlier, though little publicized, Neanderthal discoveries—such as the extensive red ochre mines of southern Africa, in use continuously from 100,000 years BP. (At one site alone, more than half a million stone digging tools were found, all showing considerable signs of wear.)

But with the publication of the *Times* article, my own status had changed dramatically. For I have maintained for the past twenty years that Neanderthals possessed a sophisticated and long-lasting civilization that was/is the source of all our so-called ancient wisdom. Abruptly, I can no longer be labeled either a crank or a fantasist—not that I ever was!

In summary, then, the position is this. Neanderthals were nocturnal in lifestyle and left-handed. They worshipped the moon, and the study of the night sky was their religion. Just like the Tamil astronomers of today, and without any mathematical notation, they could predict and study eclipses and other planetary/stellar events by manipulating rows of stones on the ground as an abacus.

Neanderthal society was ruled by women and driven by sex (whence satanism, witchcraft, and fertility religion in our own day). Since I first made that "absurd" claim, anthropologists have discovered the pygmy bonobo chimpanzees of Africa—whose society is, precisely, ruled by females and entirely driven by sex. Neanderthals built no *permanent* structures—such were anathema to them. An ornate temple built of rocks, tree trunks, and vegetation would be destroyed immediately after the relevant ceremony. Here again, no flight of fancy whatsoever is involved—for the Australian Aborigines do *precisely* this at the present day. Why did Neanderthal society worship the snake and the spider? In brief, because these are the only two species where the female is larger than the male. (The spider is also left-handed! It builds its web counterclockwise.)

The Neanderthal's consciousness was very different from our own— was much closer to what we call "dream consciousness" or the unconscious, because the Neanderthal brain differed significantly from our own. Neanderthals possessed a much larger cerebellum and a relatively smaller cerebrum, minus much of the frontal lobes that are our own trademark. The cerebellum, in ourselves, is still nevertheless the source of dreaming, of mediumistic trance, of paranormal abilities such as dowsing and telepathy, of multiple personality, of hypnotic trance, and much else besides (though you will not find these statements in conventional psychology textbooks). It is the "Atlantis" of the nervous system.

Neanderthals, in sole charge of Europe and Africa for some 200,000 years, dealt Cro-Magnons a culture shock of immense magnitude when the latter arrived in Europe via the Middle East some 35,000 years ago. Cro-Magnons had evolved somewhere in Asia—we do not yet know where— and emphatically *not* in Africa. Yet actually the culture shock, dramatic though it was, was still not the main event. The main event was the entirely fortuitous mixing of Neanderthal and Cro-Magnon genes (on something like a 10 to 90 percent relative basis), which produced the extraordinarily gifted hybrid that is ourselves.

These hybrids, true modern humans, could and would have at once begun—and in a sense did begin—to create modern civilization as we know it today. But as Graham Hancock has so well described and documented in *Fingerprints of the Gods,* there now followed a period of many thousands of years of almost unbelievable and sudden climatic and geological upheavals. Siberia, for example, was transformed from a lush temperate zone to the frozen bleakness we know today almost overnight.

Again and again, I consider, our direct ancestors' repeated attempts to produce modern civilization were brought to nothing by the onset of ice ages, of floods, of widespread volcanic eruptions and earthquakes (thus perished the Minoan civilization, for example). In this *general* sense, "lost world" scenarios are realities. Yes, the Sphinx is at least 10,000 years old. Yes, seafarers did map the coast of Antarctica many thousands of years ago. But the true ancient wisdom and the "cities of dreams" are far, far older. It was Neanderthal who mapped our skies.

The material contained in the foregoing article does not require any further comment. We have already discussed the items in detail in the earlier parts of the book.

Appendix 2
Becoming a Medium

WHAT FOLLOWS IS THE preface that I wrote in 2003 for the new edition of *The Paranormal*, republished then as an e-book by Crow Street Press in America.

In the late 1990s, in the process of changing apartments, I opened various boxes and cases that had not been touched for many years. In one of them I found a diary I had kept of the period I had spent in Coventry—actually, it had been Birmingham—when I developed as a medium. I had totally forgotten the existence of this diary.

Now I was able to read about my first paranormal experience, the *details* of which I had, again, completely forgotten.

The presiding medium at the séance where I myself first went into trance state had approached me with a "message." She was speaking in trance in the voice of her Chinese guide. In her outstretched hands I saw an open golden book—a psychic vision; because, of course, in reality her hands were empty. This phenomenon, along with the message itself—see below for full detail—was, I think, a clear indication of my later career as a writer. At the time, however, I had no thought or intention whatsoever of writing books, and the fact that I subsequently completely forgot this incident is evidence enough of my indifference to that scenario. I did not, in fact, begin my writing career for another ten years.

Here now begins the actual text of the diary. Forensic testing would, of course, show that the diary was, in fact, written in 1957.

Brian had at last suggested that I attend a circle, to be held at his home on Tuesday evening, to see, as he put it, "what *can* be done." The irony of these words was lost on both of us.

Brian's father keeps a general grocery and produce store. The building was originally an inn and is some hundreds of years old. Mr. Nicholas has converted part of it into a storefront, and the family lives in the remainder. The living room I was shown into, and where the séance was to take place, was the old bar. It has a low-timbered ceiling and the remains of a big wooden inglenook fireplace. A room with a past and an atmosphere, just right, I thought, for a spiritualist séance.

I had arrived sharp at seven as requested. The store was still open, and Mr. Nicholas was serving. Brian was out fetching one or two of the other people who were to be present. Mrs. Nicholas was in the kitchen with another guest preparing sandwiches. She is a very likeable woman, forthright and unaffected, big of frame with a hint of gaunt-ness, and extremely capable. She reminds me very much of Marjorie Maine as Ma Kettle. Mr. Nicholas, on the other hand, is a rather shy man who says very little, and when he does he says it very briefly.

Both the Nicholases are spiritualists, both mediumistic. I don't think either of them ever operates as a medium, but they have certain psy-chic gifts and are very useful members of a developing circle, where they are said to be able to "lend power" to the medium leading the circle. Most mediums are the sons or daughters of other mediums or psychically gifted people, which is at once logical and suspicious, depending how you look at it. The mother of Joan Grant (who wrote *Time Out of Mind*), for instance, foresaw the sinking of the *Titanic* and canceled the family's reservations. She also foresaw the collapse of a house they were having built and just managed to get all the work-men out before the roof fell in.

It was getting on for eight o'clock when Brian eventually returned with the other participants. These included Bob and Anna (a young married couple I had already met at a party—I like both of them—Anna, incidentally, is Scots and a strict Baptist), Mrs. Kite (the medium in charge of the circle), and another lad plus two dogs whose names I have forgotten. Doreen was not to be present—apparently she had of late been bringing a disharmony into the circle. Actually, I think there was an element of small-mindedness involved here, which I did not like to see, because up till now everything had been so open and above board.

In ones and twos, we drifted into the living room. Mr. Nicholas was shutting up shop, and every so often someone would slip away and get lost for five minutes, so that getting settled in took us some time.

We were grouped in a rough circle, men and women seated alternately. The mediums—Mrs. Kite and Brian, that is—were sitting on ordinary hard straight-backed chairs with their backs to a small television light, the only illumination in the room apart from the glow of an oil-heater and the light from a tiny altar and crucifix that Mrs. Kite had brought along. Some of the others were seated in easy chairs. I, on a hard chair, sat facing the mediums, with Anna on my left side and a Mrs. Jones on my right. We had to sit with uncrossed legs and arms, both feet firmly on the floor. Brian took his shoes off, and later so did Mrs. Kite. This is apparently a normal practice among mediums.

Mrs. Kite opened the proceedings with a few words on spiritualism generally, because several of those present had never attended a circle or church meeting before. She followed her introduction with a short prayer and then asked us to sing the hymn "Healing Light," which we did. She now proposed to begin the evening proper with clairvoyance, and took her stand in the center of the circle.

She turned first to the woman whose name I have forgotten and spoke to her at some length—the details being largely of concern only to the woman herself. Mrs. Kite said finally that around the woman was quite a throng of helping spirits. (I tried hard to see them too, without success. Brian told me later that you never see when you are straining to see; it comes of itself or not at all. I had retrospective proof of this the next day.) Indeed, she felt that this woman had some psychic gifts and suggested she join one of her development circles.

I am ashamed to admit that I was actually angry and jealous that such a foolish old woman should have such interesting things said about her, while the young, clever, high-minded seeker-after-truth (me!) should be left out in the cold. I had cause soon enough to feel even more ashamed.

"The light now comes bobbing over to this young gentleman," said Mrs. Kite, turning to me. What followed was at some length and repetitious, so that I am giving only a summary. But part of it I give word for word.

It appeared that by reason of my high intelligence and other qualities, a group of learned spirits had gathered about me and were to make me the receptacle for their learning. Mrs. Kite specified a few of them—the leader an Arab, another a man of forty-five or so "the manner of whose passing was not particularly pleasant or quick" but who now returned full of vigor to carry on his interrupted work. It was now that I realized it was no longer the voice of Mrs. Kite I could hear but the voice of an old Chinese man. Mrs. Kite was now an old, bowed figure, her hands tucked inside the sleeves of an imaginary gown, swaying and nodding and smiling. Mrs. Kite's Chinese guide had assumed control.

"You have great gifts, my friend. I come here tonight in person to tell you this. You have much work to do. . . . You are very sensitive. You have a mind that seeks always the truth and is satisfied with nothing else. You will have setbacks, there will be difficulties, but they will not stop you"—now more excited—"Other men speak at second-hand, but you will speak from experience."

At this point I saw an open golden book in Mrs. Kite's outstretched hands.

"Men will listen to you because you speak from experience and not as other men do at second-hand. You will see what you wish to see. Soon you will be taken over for the work you have to do. You are very sensitive. I see around you a light that is not of this Earth. Tonight I place the precious gift of understanding in your hands"—holding out cupped hands to me—"Use it carefully. And now I must leave you, my friend. God bless you."

Mrs. Kite straightened from her bent position and, turning to another member of the circle, resumed her normal voice.

I was naturally shaken and excited by what I had heard. But not quite to the extent one might imagine, because much of what had been said had been in my mind for some years. "Seeker after truth" was my image of myself—and in this respect I saw myself as unlike other people.

The clairvoyance continued, and after a while the thoughts ceased whirling about in my head, so that I was able to take stock again of what was happening. Outside the two dogs barked fitfully. Brian was seated bolt upright and stock-still in his chair, with eyes closed, and had been thus for some time. I heard it whispered that Grey Hawk was waiting, but Mrs. Kite continued the clairvoyance in order, I imagine, that no one might feel overlooked. Anna, it appeared, might develop as a psychometrist.

As I sat there, I felt my head swimming a little, which I put down to the closeness of the room and the general excitement. This feeling passed, but then a little later the sensation returned, more strongly. I felt rather as if inside my head the heel of somebody's hand was pressing down on my brain above the left eye. Then my eyes screwed themselves tight shut of their own volition, and my head was forced forward and down and twisted to one side. With a jerk I pulled myself together. My only thought was that my subconscious was inducing pseudo-psychic symptoms—doubtless in response to my jealousy of the old woman earlier that evening. Not content with the wonderful promises that had just been made to me, I also wanted a finger in the pie of mediumship. I was angry with myself for my despicable behavior. I told myself that if I really had any mediumistic powers, then this would have been noticed by Mrs. Kite or one of the mediums in church and my attention drawn to them. Satisfied that my analysis of the situation was correct, I now gave my full attention to the proceedings again. My head cleared completely, and I was wide awake once more.

Mrs. Kite had now spoken to everyone, and we all expected Brian's part in the séance to begin. But Mr. Nicholas had to go out to quiet the dogs (animals are said to be able to sense the presence of spirits) and to make sure that no one was trying to break into the shop. So we waited for him to return.

After a few moments, Mrs. Kite turned to me again. "There's a young man here in air force uniform killed in the last war. Can you place him?" I said it might be a cousin of mine. "He is with a group of other young fellows, laughing and joking. At first he was very bitter about his death, but he is happy now. He is a very intelligent spirit and has already developed considerably."

The details fitted perfectly for my cousin. He was highly intelligent. He was recently married and not long before his death had become a father. His family, unlike mine, was very wealthy, so the world was more or less at his feet when he was killed, which would account for the bitterness. I had myself always regretted his death (when I was eleven) because I was drawn to him and would have liked to get to know him. (I never had that feeling about any of my other relatives.)

"He is trying to take control of me," went on Mrs. Kite. "But I mustn't let him. He wants you to know that he has been near you and knows about you. He says you have had a cough recently." Now I had had for the past two weeks a persistent cough, unusual for me, and so persistent was it that I was considering going for a chest X-ray. "He says you are shortly to do a course of study, and he will help you with it." This referred, of course, to the Dip. Ed., which I am to do next October. *Nobody present knew anything of this.*

"These things he tells you to prove that he knows about you." (The items concerned—including the air force uniform—are, of course, extremely evidentiary. No one could argue coincidence with regard to all this detail.) "He speaks of a man who has had an operation for stomach trouble." I said this must be my father (who has cancer of the pancreas). "He speaks of a lady who has some trouble here"—laying her hand on her right side. I said this might be my mother (she has pains everywhere). "He sends his love to his parents—and has he a sister?" (A medium is not supposed to ask probing questions like this.) "Yes." "He sends her his love too. He wants you to take his love to them."

Mr. Nicholas had now returned, and Mrs. Kite turned to Brian. "We have someone here who has been waiting to speak to us." Brian, who had not moved a muscle for about an hour, shuddered a little, grunted once or twice—and then the deep, harsh voice of an American Indian said: "Good evening, friends."

This voice was much more convincing than that of Mrs. Kite's Chinese man. There was only the faintest suspicion of Brian's own voice about it. (Spiritualists readily agree that there is sometimes a touch of the medium's own voice in a speaking spirit—as I have remarked elsewhere, there is no suspension of critical faculty among spiritualists. The quality of the voice and accent depends on the depth of trance and the state of development of the medium concerned.)

"Oh, hello, Grey Hawk," said Mrs. Nicholas chattily and casually, as if speaking to a neighbor who had dropped in for a cup of tea. "Please sing a hymn," said Grey Hawk. His insistence on a hymn was, I think, for the benefit of those of us who were new, lest they might think this the work of the devil or in some way irreligious and frivolous. We sang "The Lord Is My Shepherd." Still chatting, Mrs. Nicholas went on after this about the noise the dogs were making. "Yes," said Grey Hawk. "We tried to quiet them." A few more pleasantries, and then Grey Hawk began to address a sort of sermon to the circle. He was saying something about "We now rise to the upper spheres where God is present" when quite suddenly and without warning, something began that was undoubtedly the most wonderful thing that has ever happened to me. It is not easy to put it into words.

A wave of sensation swept through me, which made me take a deep gasping breath. My brain spun wildly. With triumphant excitement, I realized that I was being "controlled." After an initial sensation of soaring upward, I was now falling. Then the feeling of movement ceased abruptly. My head fell back. Then, a great distance away, I could hear the long, labored breathing of a body, which I could no longer feel and to which I was attached only by a fine thread. I was nevertheless aware of the silent tension that filled the room. Then came a period of unconsciousness. When I returned to myself again, a hymn was being sung. My head was hanging down onto my chest, my hands dangled at my sides, and I was barely breathing.

Mrs. Kite was standing in front of me. "Raise your hands, Stan," she said. I gave her my hands. Then she addressed the spirit within me. "Hello. We're pleased to have you with us. Won't you speak to us, friend? Use your instrument. Use your instrument, friend." At this, my brain, which had cleared momentarily, grew very confused again. I seemed to be in charge of one half of it, and someone or something else was in charge of the other half. This other intelligence seemed to want to say "Hello" or "Good evening" or some word of greeting. But this was not achieved. Instead I groaned and fell forward.

I could hear Grey Hawk saying repeatedly: "All is well. All is well. It is very beautiful. Do not be afraid." These remarks were to the other members of the circle.

This was, I think, the high point of the trance, insofar as I was only about half in charge of my mind and my body. After this, the other influence seemed to grow weaker and weaker and to withdraw. Mrs. Kite was still urging me to speak. Grey Hawk, now speaking to me, said: "Do not be afraid, fear will harm the condition."

I was afraid, naturally, or at least what I felt was a mixture of fear and excitement. I was anxious not to be afraid, not to spoil things. It was perhaps my very desire to help, the over-interference of my conscious mind, that prevented a more successful outcome.

I heard Mr. Nicholas say: "We mustn't leave him under too long first time." Mrs. Kite now raised me from my chair and led me into the center of the circle. This is a symbolic welcome to the spirit visitor. Through half-closed eyes I glimpsed the immobile figure of Brian. A hymn was being sung. A feeling of great happiness came over me, and I was smiling and grinning. "You're very happy to be with us, aren't you?" said Mrs. Kite. And then almost immediately came a complete change. The happy mood was replaced by a terribly intense feeling of sadness, which quickly overwhelmed me, so that I broke down and sobbed in Mrs. Kite's arms as if I would never stop. They were, however, tears not only of sadness, but of gratitude and humility in the presence of something very wonderful. A period of blankness then, and I came to sobbing into my hands, and sitting in my chair.

After a while, the sadness passed, and I looked up to find Mrs. Kite in front of me, controlled again by her guide. He rocked backward and forward on his heels, beside himself with delight. "Did I not say he had great gifts? Did I not say it? He is so sensitive, so pliant. And so willing." Then he began to speak rapid Chinese. (I can't *prove* it was Chinese, of course.) He was stroking my forehead with both hands. I felt the spirit beginning to go from me completely. Finally he ran his hands down my arms and legs as if squeezing water from a sponge, and I was completely myself again—a little bewildered but very happy, my eyes and face still wet with tears.

Brian came over to me, obviously very pleased, and laughing at my expression. From all sides envious glances. "You've been holding out on us, Stan," said Mrs. Nicholas. Questions all around—was this really the first time I had sat in a circle? Had I ever had any psychic experiences before? How did I feel now? Someone asked Bob what he thought of spiritualism *now,* and he muttered something about self-hypnosis, but nobody seemed offended. Anna said that far from being frightened (she is very excitable and easily gets hysterical), she had had to suppress a desire to laugh out loud (which could be a fear reaction anyway), but again nobody was offended.

Mrs. Kite drew me to one side. "We've been looking so long for someone like you." I felt very proud that Mrs. Kite should speak to me, as it were, on equal terms. Apparently she too had been controlled at her first séance. She warned me not to "sit" alone, that is, not to allow myself to be controlled unless someone experienced were present who knew what should be done. Otherwise the consequences could be serious. In her opinion, the spirit who had attempted to control me was my cousin. "That boy will be able to help you a lot if you let him. Turn your thoughts to him when you need help."

It was now very late (about 1:30 a.m.), and one of the circle was asked to run me and another guest home in his car. I arrived back at my digs some time after 2:00 a.m., with packing for the next day still to be done, the last day of term. I was planning to catch the 4:30 p.m. train straight from school the next day. I slept hardly at all that night and went through the next day with a splitting headache and a brain that refused to focus on anything. This added greatly to the normal difficulties of the last day of any term.

The above concludes the extract from the 1957 diary. But there is one further dramatic item. A few weeks subsequently, I had a private sitting with Grey Hawk. Among other matters, he said:

You have a great future, my friend. There will be much material hardship, but you will be supported by the things of spirit. You do not dream what things will happen. You will see many things. You will be shown a great plan. But not yet—you must be patient.

The relevance and accuracy of both Mrs. Kite's and Grey Hawk's comments about my life and future cannot be overstressed.

How and why could these comments be relevant with regard to a young man working as a substitute teacher in general subjects (okay, I did have a degree in modern languages) living as a lodger (with an elderly couple) who had no idea whatsoever of what future career he wanted? (How, in fact, would such comments be relevant and appropriate even to 99 percent of the population?) And, in fact—I have never heard a medium speak in such extreme terms to anyone else. "You have great gifts" . . . "You have a mind that always seeks the truth and is satisfied with nothing else" . . . "You will have setbacks, there will be difficulties" . . . "There will be much material hardship" . . . "You will be shown a great plan."

Why, in particular, should I suffer material hardship? I had a degree and could always get a job.

But in fact, despite so much critical acclaim (see appendix 3), I actually spent much of my writing career doing odd jobs for Manpower—including cleaning bathrooms!

As for the great plan, the search for truth, the work to be done, and so forth—little did I know that I would be privileged to discover that 50 percent of our psychology is missing—or rather, it was missing. For it now exists in my books.

And, of course—it has to be said again—the open, golden book I saw in Mrs. Kite's hands remains *absolutely* remarkable.

How could that not be evidentiary?

Appendix 3

In Praise of
Stan Gooch's Work

THE FOLLOWING ARE BUT a sampling of the review quotes collected over
the many years of my writing career. They will, I trust, further encourage
students to take on the establishment—that is, their own tutors, lecturers, professors—in support of the matters presented in this book.

By the way, perhaps I should mention that following publication of my
first book *Total Man* I was given an entry in *Who's Who in the World*.

GENERAL PRAISE

"A brilliant, bold and original thinker."

ROBERT TEMPLE, AUTHOR OF
THE SIRIUS MYSTERY AND *THE GENIUS OF CHINA*

"I stand in awe of your greater scholarship."

LYALL WATSON,
AUTHOR OF *BEYOND SUPERNATURE* AND
THE NATURE OF THINGS

"Stan Gooch was the first person to state that Neanderthal man had red hair, confirmed by the Oxford Institute for Molecular biology in 2001. He was also the first to say, back in 1980, that Roger Sperry's 'split-brain' theory—for which he received the Nobel Prize—was fundamentally flawed. Sperry's theory was officially discredited by the scientific establishment in 2002."

PROGRESS

IN PRAISE OF *CITIES OF DREAMS*

"With his latest book Stan Gooch may be ready to rejoin the academic establishment as an innovator where sheer originality can no longer be ignored. *Cities of Dreams* proves that far from being an eccentric maverick Gooch is one of the world's formidable and consistent thinkers alive today."

COLIN WILSON, AUTHOR OF *ATLANTIS AND THE KINGDOM OF THE NEANDERTHALS* AND *FROM ATLANTIS TO THE SPHINX*

"Stan Gooch is a careful and passionate researcher. We need him. For we have eaten of the Tree of Knowledge but not of the Tree of Life, and as Joseph Campbell used to say, wouldn't you like a bite of that? *Cities of Dreams* is a book of daring, insight, of imagination. A book of the timeless and a book of our time."

RESEARCH INTO LOST
KNOWLEDGE ORGANISATION

IN PRAISE OF
THE DOUBLE HELIX OF THE MIND

"Relentlessly original."

STANLEY KRIPPNER, COAUTHOR OF *HEALING STATES* AND COEDITOR OF *VARIETIES OF ANOMALOUS EXPERIENCE*

"This important book will surely provoke wide-ranging debate."

SCIENCE OF THOUGHT REVIEW

IN PRAISE OF
THE DREAM CULTURE OF THE NEANDERTHALS

"The latest and most daring of evolutionary theories—so well presented that it is difficult not to be convinced."

WESTERN DAILY PRESS

"Gooch's brilliance is undeniable."

BOOKS AND BOOKMEN

IN PRAISE OF *THE NEANDERTHAL QUESTION*

"The most gripping part of his work deals with Cro-Magnon and Neanderthal Man. He writes about them as if he had just come from a television interview with several."

TIME OUT

IN PRAISE OF *THE ORIGINS OF PSYCHIC PHENOMENA*

"Gooch presents a legion of bizarre happenings, crying out to be called incredible—except that they are witnessed, documented, authenticated. The book is startling enough to upstage Stephen King and makes horror comics seem pedestrian."

DAILY MAIL

"What an interesting, crowded, maddening whirlwind of a book."

RENÉE HAYNES, *THE TABLET*

"The evidence presented is curiously compelling and the book well worth reading."

IRISH INDEPENDENT

"Frighteningly well argued."

TIMES EDUCATIONAL SUPPLEMENT

IN PRAISE OF *THE PARANORMAL*

"A book that even the sceptic can read with enjoyment and profit—not just for the converted."

BRITISH JOURNAL OF PSYCHOLOGY (*THE PARANORMAL* WAS
THE FIRST BOOK ON THAT SUBJECT EVER REVIEWED FAVORABLY
BY THE *BRITISH JOURNAL OF PSYCHOLOGY.*)

"To his credit Gooch insists upon approaching the paranormal on its own terms—terms radically different from those proposed by investigation of the orthodox scientists. But the primary value of Gooch's vision lies in his ability to advance and inspire the reader."

SINGULARITIES

"Stan Gooch is a splendid advocate of the open-minded approach to the world lying beyond our ordinary sense."

MANCHESTER EVENING NEWS

IN PRAISE OF
PERSONALITY AND EVOLUTION

"An abstract does no justice to the richness of material, live writing and exceptionally clear thinking which Stan Gooch commands."

JACQUETTA HAWKES, *SUNDAY TIMES*
(*PERSONALITY AND EVOLUTION* WAS MADE ONE OF THE NINE
"BOOKS OF THE YEAR" IN THE *SUNDAY TIMES.*)

"We cannot but admire Stan Gooch's massive and challenging endeavor."

LOS ANGELES TIMES

IN PRAISE OF *THE SECRET LIFE OF HUMANS*

"Gooch boldly recalls our attention to the fact that man—in nature, society, history—is such a many-sided being that to lose this vision is to place ourselves in real peril—that we must put into proper perspective the recent 'authority' of science."

NEW HUMANIST

"A wealth of examples—fascinating case after fascinating case—both intriguing and impressive."

DUMFRIES AND GALLOWAY EXPRESS

"Like yourself I have been trying to make sense of experiences that are consistently devalued by mainstream science. Your admirable summaries have given me the courage to take some steps forward."

PETER REDGROVE,
COAUTHOR OF *THE WISE WOUND*

IN PRAISE OF *TOTAL MAN*

"One of the most exciting and original thinkers to appear in many years."

BOOKS AND BOOKMEN

"Drawing on literature and legend, on science fiction and mythology, history, physiology, psychology, linguistics and art, British psychologist Stan Gooch has written a daring new interpretation of the human psyche. *Total Man,* which contains what may be the best defense of the I Ching as a way of knowledge since Carl Jung, presents a rare attempt at providing a complete system of thought aimed at fostering the evolution of a 'new consciousness.'"

PUBLISHER'S WEEKLY

"[Stan Gooch's] vision of duality is arresting and his exploration will fascinate layman and scholar alike."

LIBRARY JOURNAL

PRAISE FROM MY READERS

More than one of the foregoing quotes implies that important items are missing from our existing scenario and that my books alone deal with these. That position is further reinforced by the following extracts from some of the many letters that my readers have been kind enough to send me over the years:

"Your style, wit and intelligence are marvelous. You are one of the few wise writers in print today. Us Neanderthal nerds need our dose of Gooch every two or three years and you're the only one that can supply it."

E.G.

"I wish to thank you for the enormous help you have given me in your writings. I have studied many great thinkers—Freud, Jung, Fromm, Reich—but you have it *all* together. Again much gratitude."

J.F.-W.

Letter sent to all Chief Librarians:

"I have just recently been trying to obtain books by Stan Gooch from public libraries but was not a little dismayed by the lack of comprehensive coverage of his work. This man is a true, towering genius whose work in psychology, language and the origins of man has been ground breaking. But the received wisdom of academics at this point in history is to completely ignore him."

G.C.D.

"Myself and several colleagues are passionate followers of your work."

J.L., MARION FOUNDATION

"I was very impressed with *Cities of Dreams,* as indeed I have been with all your previous works, having read everything from *Total Man* onwards. It is impossible to read your books without feeling that the answers to human origins and destiny are about to be revealed on the next page. This at a time when increasingly if I start to read one book I feel I should be reading something else."

J.C.

"I stumbled across your book *Cities of Dreams* some four or five months ago, and read it over the Easter period with an almost unbearable excitement. When I reached the end I did something I have never done before—I turned straight back to the beginning and started over again. I am currently reading it for the third time, sharing it in all its detail with my analyst. I am also very excited with your style of writing, with the passion of your presentation of the facts and ideas, the openness and humour of your partisanship, the way you emphasize the most horrific factual discoveries and acknowledge your feeling reaction to them."

R.G.

So there you are, students.

Selected Bibliography

Alexander, H. B., ed. *The Mythology of All Races*. New York: Cooper Square, 1964.

Ashe, Geoffrey. *The Ancient Wisdom*. London: Macmillan, 1977.

Bayanov, Dmitri, and Igor Bourtsev. "On Neanderthal vs Paranthropus." *Current Anthropology* 17 (June 1976).

Briffault, Robert. *The Mothers: A Study of the Origins of Sentiments and Institutions*. London: Macmillan, 1927.

Brown, Peter Lancaster. *Megaliths, Myths and Men*. Mineola, N.Y.: Dover Publications, 2000.

Burl, Aubrey. *The Stone Circles of the British Isles*. London: Yale University Press, 1976.

Eiseley, Loren. *The Unexpected Universe*. London: Gollancz, 1970.

Freud, Sigmund. *The Interpretation of Dreams*. London: Allen & Unwin, 1954.

Gooch, Stan. *The Dream Culture of the Neanderthals*. Rochester, Vt.: Inner Traditions, 2006.

———. *The Neanderthal Question*. London: Wildwood House, 1977.

———. *Personality and Evolution*. London: Wildwood House, 1973.

———. *Total Man*. London: Allen Lane, 1972.

Goodman, Geoffrey. *Psychic Archaeology*. New York: Putnam, 1977.

Grossman, S. P. *A Textbook of Physiological Psychology*. New York: Wiley, 1967.

Guirand, Felix. *New Larousse Encyclopedia of Mythology*. London: Hamlyn, 1969.

Harlow, H. F. "Love in Infant Monkeys." *Scientific American,* June 1959.

Heyerdahl, Thor. *Aku, Aku: The Secret of Easter Island*. London: Allen & Unwin, 1958.

Hitching, Francis. *The World Atlas of Mysteries*. London: Collins, 1978.

Hulse, Frederick S. *The Human Species*. New York: Random House, 1971.

Jobes, Gertrude. *Dictionary of Mythology, Folklore and Symbols*. New York: Scarecrow, 1961.

Jolly, Alison. *The Evolution of Primate Behaviour*. London: Macmillan, 1972.

Jung, C. G. *Flying Saucers: A Modern Myth*. London: Routledge, 1977.

Lacey, Louise. *Lunaception*. New York: Warner, 1976.

Lethbridge, T. C. *Witches: Investigating an Ancient Religion*. London: Routledge, 1962.

Murray, Margaret. *The God of the Witches*. London: Faber, 1952.

———. *The Witch Cult in Western Europe*. London: Oxford University Press, 1962.

Needham, Rodney. *Right and Left*. Chicago: University of Chicago Press, 1973.

Porshnev, B. F. "The Troglodytidae and the Hominidae in the Taxonomy and Evolution of Higher Primates." *Current Anthropology* 15 (1974).

Radford, E., and M. A. Radford. *Encyclopedia of Superstitions*. Edited by Christina Hole. London: Hutchinson, 1961.

Redgrove, Peter, and Penelope Shuttle. *The Terrors of Dr. Treviles*. London: Routledge, 1974.

Russell, Jeffrey Burton. *Witchcraft in the Middle Ages*. New York: Cornell University, 1972.

Sandars, N. K. *Prehistoric Art in Europe*. Harmondsworth, U.K.: Penguin, 1968.

Shackley, Myra. *Still Living? Yeti, Sasquatch and the Neanderthal Enigma*. New York: W. W. Norton & Company, 1986.

Shuttle, Penelope, and Peter Redgrove. *The Wise Wound*. London: Gollancz, 1978.

Skeat, W. W. *An Etymological Dictionary of the English Language*. London: Oxford University Press, 1946.

Smith, Don. *Why Are There Gays at All?* London: Quantum Jump Publications, 1978.

Solecki, Ralph S. *Shanidar: The Humanity of Neanderthal Man.* London: Allen Lane, 1972.

————. "Shanidar IV, a Neanderthal Flower Burial in Northern Iraq." *Science* 190 (1975).

Sparks, John. *Bird Behavior.* London: Hamlyn, 1969.

Spengler, Oswald. *Man and Technics.* London: Allen & Unwin, 1932.

Stephens, W. N. *The Family in Cross-Cultural Perspective.* New York: Holt, 1963.

Swedenborg, Emmanuel. *Heaven and Hell.* London: Swedenborg Society, 1896.

Targ, Russell, and Harold Puthof. *Mind-Reach.* London: Paladin, 1978.

Temple, Robert. *The Sirius Mystery.* London: Sidgwick & Jackson, 1976.

Teng, E. L., et al. "Handedness in a Chinese Population." *Science* 193 (1976).

Vlcek, Emanuel. "Old Literary Evidence for the Existence of the 'Snow Man' in Tibet and Mongolia." *Man* 59 (1959).

Yerkes, R. M., and A. W. Yerkes. *The Great Apes.* London: Yale University Press, 1929.

Zerchaninov, Yuri. "Is Neanderthal Man Extinct?" *Moscow News,* 22 February 1964.

Index

BOOKS OF RELATED INTEREST

The Dream Culture of the Neanderthals
Guardians of the Ancient Wisdom
by Stan Gooch

The Origins of Psychic Phenomena
Poltergeists, Incubi, Succubi, and the Unconscious Mind
by Stan Gooch

Atlantis and the Kingdom of the Neanderthals
100,000 Years of Lost History
by Colin Wilson

From the Ashes of Angels
The Forbidden Legacy of a Fallen Race
by Andrew Collins

Gods of Eden
Egypt's Lost Legacy and the Genesis of Civilization
by Andrew Collins

Forbidden History
Prehistoric Technologies, Extraterrestrial Intervention, and the Suppressed
Origins of Civilization
Edited by J. Douglas Kenyon

The Science of the Dogon
Decoding the African Mystery Tradition
by Laird Scranton

The Sirius Mystery
New Scientific Evidence of Alien Contact 5,000 Years Ago
by Robert Temple

Inner Traditions • Bear & Company
P.O. Box 388
Rochester, VT 05767
1-800-246-8648
www.InnerTraditions.com
Or contact your local bookseller